DAVID HICKS
MY KIND OF GARDEN

from Frieda & Alex
on my 47th birthday
April 2005

DAVID HICKS
MY KIND OF GARDEN

EDITED BY ASHLEY HICKS

PHOTOGRAPHS BY DANA HYDE

GARDEN * ART * PRESS

ACKNOWLEDGEMENTS

Many people have helped with the production of this book, both during the time my father worked on it and since his death. I must crave their indulgence for the most part in being unable to thank them individually. I can only say what a pleasure it is to have this last piece of his work finished.

I would like to thank particularly Graham Viney, Paul Bangay and Madison Cox, who were very helpful with South Africa, Australia and the United States respectively; Diana Steel of the Antique Collectors' Club who had the vision and the perseverance to publish this book; and of course Dana Hyde Scrymgeour whose marvellous photographs and infinite patience made my father's idea a reality.

With the complications of producing this book from my father's unfinished copy, minor errors or omissions may have crept in and, if so, I must ask for the understanding of the gardens' owners.

Finally, I should thank my darling wife, who has put up with rather more of her late father-in-law's gardening tastes than she might have expected; and my mother, living surrounded by the beauty of The Grove, who made me promise to finish Papa's book even before he had left the house.

Ashley Hicks

Frontispiece: White painted trunks in the Provençal manner at Le Clos Fiorentina, France.
Title page: Plywood pyramid designed by David Hicks.

©1999 The Estate of David Hicks
World copyright reserved

ISBN 1 870673 48 4

First published 1999
Reprinted 2000, 2004
Paperback edition first published 2003
Reprinted 2004

The right of David Hicks to be identified as author of this work has been asserted by his executors
in accordance with the Copyright, Designs and Patents Act 1988.

British Library Cataloguing-in-Publication Data:
a catalogue record for this book is available from the British Library.

Printed in China for Garden Art Press,
Old Martlesham, Woodbridge, Suffolk, IP12 4SD

CONTENTS

When David Hicks asked me some time ago to write a foreword to his book, I felt extremely flattered and was delighted to comply. I have always had the greatest respect for David's skills as a designer of interiors, from my own first set of rooms at Buckingham Palace, years ago now, to his varied commissions that I have seen over the years. I have also admired, like many people, the little paradise of a garden that he created at The Grove, with its wonderful sense of drama that fills every new vista or garden "room". Every now and then I used to spot it from the air from a helicopter, such was its noticeable character...

What was always fascinating about David, and is well reflected in this book, was his very catholic taste in other people's gardens. He held strict, rigid views about many things, but delighted in the most surprising creations of other people - including, I was pleased to learn, my own!

After the desperately sad news of David's death last year, I was relieved to hear that this book was still to go ahead. Its wide range of gardens, geographic and historical, mirrors his personal love of travel and his vast knowledge of the past. The book will, I hope, be enjoyed by everyone who shares a love of gardens and the spirit of creativity and inspiration which they represent. I hope it will also be a lasting reminder to many people of what a remarkably talented person David was. We shall miss him hugely...

Facing. The temple and stumpwork at Highgrove.

XXX
VIII
MCM XC

I am pulsating with ideas. No more weeds
no more last minute infilling with easy
colour from Brazil but a plan to
re-create the citrus, camellia and rose
collections, to get the main gardens
and terraces looking stylish and to
incorporate new features — rooms of
plant material by colour and by scent.

Tunnels of Wisteria, walls of Jasmine,
fountains of different water sounds.
Surprises, drama, imagination & contrast
of texture. But nothing too elaborate.
Seats, pavilions, sunk rose gardens,
Sedums in pots — every stylish
ingenuity that can be imagined for
that sublime site. Simple elegance.

You have made the house so very super—
let's now get the outside right too.

I will take a possessive interest in the
entire project and will instruct and
supervise as much as is required.

David Hicks

David Hicks wrote this 'philosophy of design' in a letter to a prospective client, 1990.

Facing. The Rose Tunnel at The Grove.

A GARDENING CHILDHOOD

When I was about six years old, my best friends were Doris Mills, the cook, Mabel Goult, the house parlourmaid, and Frank Sapsford, the gardener.

Although I had a doting mother, she played bridge every afternoon five days a week and my father went every day to the Stock Exchange. On Saturdays in the winter he shot from dawn to dusk and on Sunday mornings he would spend hours in his hothouses before Doctor Turner came for sherry at midday. After lunch he would read until Evensong.

My dear brother John and I were great friends and would often go riding together but he was seven years older than me and I was left very much on my own, particularly when he was called up. Consequently I spent hours with Sapsford in the garden, watching and chatting.

When I was eight I was given my own small piece of garden and six months later I was packed off to a preparatory school in Surrey with a tuck box and a brand new spade, fork, rake and hoe to 'Dig for Victory!'

In my early teens my mother and I would often go to see the gardens of friends in the neighbourhood of Coggeshall. Scripps had its avenue of Lombardy poplars, planted in memory of Colonel Hancock's fellow officers in the Coldstream Guards who were killed in the First World War. Felix Hall boasted sphinxes and statuary against a lush background of Lebanon cedars. Prested Hall was characterised by its bright planting and the blue Atlantic cedars which I was later to realise were the favourite trees of the *nouveaux riches*. Other friends of my mother all had gardens with distinctive styles and I was already unknowingly beginning to form my own taste which was later to develop into a strong streak of snobbery about garden layout and plants. Mrs. Morrison's garden had a studied middle class look, whilst those of Geoffrey Holmes and Sir Cedric Morris had a distinctly bold and romantic feel.

In 1945, when I was sixteen, we moved from Essex to Sudbury, Suffolk, and I

With my pony Tuppence, spring 1937.

With my brother and mother, 1936.

designed the plan for the new garden. My mother and I chose all the plants at local nurseries. I was hooked.

Art school and conscription followed Charterhouse. I became the youngest member of the Georgian Group and with them visited many great houses not then open to the public. My one really powerful memory is of going to Sissinghurst in my Royal Army Education Corps sergeant's uniform and sketching there. Seated on my small stool I suddenly saw in front of me a distinctive pair of brown lace-up boots and riding breeches. It was Vita Sackville-West. "What's a soldier doing drawing my garden?", she asked. "You'd better come up to my tower to see the layout from there and we'll have some tea".

I will attempt to explain elsewhere what I have learnt from the gardens and designers who influenced me. I now come to describe how I became a garden designer after spending twenty-six years as a designer of interiors, fabrics, carpets and furniture.

After my first simple plan for our garden in Suffolk in 1945, my next garden was created in 1956 when I rented The Temple at Stoke by Nayland, also in Suffolk.

The Temple was built in the manner of Sir Robert Taylor in about 1755 as a fishing pavilion for the Rowleys. Standing at the top of a large formal canal bordered by two hundred-year-old Spanish chestnuts, it needed a frame on either side and at the back. Taking John Fowler's hornbeam stilt tree idea, I added a hornbeam hedge under and just behind it and planted these either side of the house, thus creating my first two green rooms which I filled with roses.

In 1960 I created another garden, this time for my wife and myself – Britwell Salome with staggering views of rolling Oxfordshire country and which I made famous with my new look of modern living in a classical setting. It was a wonderful rose garden in a walled area. In 1980, however, we sold Britwell. We had enjoyed twenty luxurious years there but could no longer afford to continue living in such a large house. We kept most of the land and moved into The Grove.

In the garden pond with my dog, 1936.

My mother and her pug, 1938.

Frank Sapsford with my brother John and me, 1936.

INFLUENCES
AND INSPIRATIONS

I believe that all creative people seek inspiration from the past; those that don't, perhaps should. At seventeen I went to Versailles and was staggered by Le Nôtre – by the sense of scale which impressed and influenced me immensely – not that I ever expected to be fortunate enough to work on a project of such majestic proportions; it was a great lesson in scale. Then I went to Provence and saw his work above the Roman baths at Nîmes which is supremely simple but the same mastery of scale is again evident. Later, in Italy, I discovered the marvels and excitements of that country's Renaissance and Mannerist gardens.

I am so passionate about design, formality, straight lines, symmetry, that I find almost tragic the work of Capability Brown who destroyed so many fine avenues and marvellous English gardens, many inspired very directly by the Italian gardens visited by the Grand Tourists, in order to make the idyllic parkland look of the 'classic English garden'. Brown was succeeded by Humphry Repton and he in turn by Loudon and then Robinson. All Romantics.

From the late 19th century on, the growth of the picturesque, with the herbaceous border as King, was to my mind a vulgar decay. There are few things worse than the horrors of municipal flower-planting, which has evolved frighteningly out of the gardens of a more luxurious era. It is with a sigh of relief that I welcome the new gardening ideas of the 20th century. I relish formal garden design in the way that Inigo Triggs interpreted formal design around 1913, and later Geoffrey Jellicoe. Lutyens was a great garden architect who, with and without Gertrude Jekyll, was interpreting formal design with his own very original style.

I have been very influenced and inspired by Sissinghurst, by Hidcote and by the Hunting Lodge at Odiham. All three were designed by men: Harold Nicolson, Lawrence Johnston and John Fowler. The Moghul Garden behind Viceroy's House at New Delhi, Blagdon and Hestercombe, Tyringham and Folly Farm all show Lutyens's genius. Russell Page, Geoffrey Jellicoe, Harold Peto were all great designers and back the list goes: Bridgeman, Le Nôtre, de Caus.

All these designers were men, but I do have the greatest admiration for those wonderful female plantsmen like Edith Wharton, Gertrude Jekyll and, more recently, Nancy Lancaster, Lady Salisbury, Rosemary Verey, Penelope Hobhouse and Arabella Lennox-Boyd.

I am permanently in a state of transition because I do not want my garden, or my garden design for my clients, to stand still. I myself have no pretensions to being a plantsman; I like decisive design and those plants that I really love. Influence is always there to be referred to, and although my ideas are firmly established I am always open minded about considering new influences.

One of the upper terraces at Vignola's great palace, Villa Farnese, Caprarola. The simplicity of the design, of low green walls of hedge surrounded by bearded stone terms, is breathtaking.

ITALIAN GARDENS
VILLA FARNESE, CAPRAROLA
VILLA LANTE, BAGNAIA
VILLA GAMBERAIA, SETTIGNANO

I first saw many of the Italian gardens in the early 1950s when, as an impressionable young art student, I toured Italy, painting what I saw in brightly coloured, very linear gouaches. The excitement that I felt then has not left me and my heart still leaps at the beauty and, so often, the surprise of these gardens. I love the formality, the strong lines, the theatre of them, their sense of scale, and above all their lack of colour. I have always found colossally inspiring this architecture of green leaf, of stone and painted plaster, and of the running water that cools and refreshes in the heat of an Italian summer

For me, the best gardens of Italy are those intended for private enjoyment and entertaining, not for public display.

The famous water chain that connects the upper and lower parts of the Vignola garden at Villa Lante. The icy coolness of the rushing water forms the central axis of this, to my mind, the most perfect of the Italian gardens.

* It looks elaborate but it can be made of painted concrete.

Sketch for a fountain inspired by those I have seen in Italy.

The house is often a simple retreat, as here at Villa Gamberaia, with an asymmetric façade to the symmetric garden.

I love the simplicity of this wall that bounds the upper terrace at Gamberaia, with its plain, curved pedestals topped with urns and animals.

The ornamental potager at Villandry is a splendid creation, both in overall effect and detail.
The sixteen rose arbours in the centre are a contrast to the symmetry of the planting and I always feel
pleased to see juxtapositions like this.

VILLANDRY
TOURS, FRANCE

I find each visit to Villandry more exciting than the last. For me this is one of the seven wonders of the world, with its enveloping sense of green architecture, the broad expanse of the Clos d'Eau, the pollarded limes, and the clipped hornbeam walls. But there is also, in complete contrast, the beautifully reconstructed 16th century vegetable and flower garden, like something from the *Très Riches Heures du Duc de Berry*, brought stunningly to life. Villandry, in the rolling landscape of Touraine, more than any other great garden, can give ideas for large, medium and small gardens. What pleases me most is the true and totally disciplined sense of tonal gardening – green on green on green.

Immaculately trimmed box hedges in the Garden of Love.

Facing. As replanted in the early 20th century, the garden at Villandry has had an enormous influence on my work.

17

CHATEAU DE BRECY
ST. GABRIEL-BRECY, FRANCE

At the Château de Brécy in northern France, my French associate Barbara Wirth, with her husband Didier, found the bones of a magnificent Baroque garden designed by Jules-Hardouin Mansart, the architect of Versailles. Over a number of years, they have painstakingly restored the garden, with its hugely complex parterres and terraces, to the glories of its 17th century origins.

One of a fine pair of double-headed lions guarding the château.

Facing. The stepped terraces seen from the château. The perspective continues beyond the gates of the formal garden and into the countryside.

Containers should make a statement as to where they are placed. The large blue 'Versailles' tubs against the rough stone wall, mirrored by smaller tubs against the box hedge, and fruit and flower basket finials on top of the wall – all are perfectly positioned.

The magnificent gates at the Château de Brécy looking towards the château from the terraced grounds.

Facing. Amongst the rigid formality of the classical garden at Brécy, an enchanting surprise in the shape of a Gothic arch with rambling, natural planting.

20

HET LOO PALACE
APELDOORN, THE NETHERLANDS

This extraordinary garden, recently restored by a very enlightened Dutch government, was created by the Frenchman Daniel Marot in 1692 for William and Mary at their Dutch palace following their joint accession to the English throne. Similar gardens were created at Hampton Court, Kensington and elsewhere but this is the only true survivor of this style of garden, and as such gives a glimpse of how the first large-scale classical gardens in England must have looked.

A glimpse into the garden through dramatic gates.

Facing. The Great Garden, created in 1692 out of rivalry with the Versailles of Louis XIV, whom William loathed.

The 'berceau' of the Queen's Garden at Het Loo seen from the roof of the palace.

One of the pleasures of being a garden designer is discovering surprises like this imaginative topiary arrangement inside the 'berceau'.

Facing. The elaborate Baroque 'Parterres de Broderie' in the Queen's Garden next to the palace. The contrast of the complex design with the simplicity of the obelisks and tubs is marvellous.

24

Inside the trellis-framed 'berceau', long
corridors with windows turn corners with
deep Baroque curves.

Facing. A wonderfully small-scale view
in a huge-scale garden through an
arched window in the trellis 'berceau'.

26

CHISWICK HOUSE

LONDON, ENGLAND

This is a magical garden, full of superb statuary, which I first saw as a very young man. It was laid out by William Kent in the 1730s and 1740s, and I feel a certain affinity with Kent, for he was a painter, decorator and furniture designer before he turned architect and garden designer. At Chiswick, Kent and Lord Burlington initiated a plan which followed the formal fashion for gardens of the time while introducing features that were less geometrically arranged and included many serpentine twists and turns. Among the gems are the curving close-cut hedging of the Exedra with statuary, long tree-lined vistas, and the perfect little Orange Tree Garden with its domed and porticoed temple, circular pool, obelisk and turfed amphitheatre.

The Orange Tree Garden surrounded by an elegant stepped turf amphitheatre.

BAGATELLE
PARIS, FRANCE

This charming pavilion and grounds in the Bois de Boulogne was built in 1777 for Louis XVI's brother the Comte d'Artois (later Charles X). Although the original French formal garden at the rear has been greatly modified the present parterre is still evocative.

In the early 19th century garden of old roses nearby, broad gravel paths wind through lawns edged with closely trimmed box and yew. The classical forms of old-fashioned roses, from the purity of the Dog Rose to the luxurious opulence of the Cabbage Rose, and the blowsy, heady Damask Rose, are what real roses are all about: rich, exuberant, superbly balanced and fragrant. In comparison, I find many modern roses, dull, flat, lacking both in quality and scent.

The gem-like pavilion seen through an arch of massed rambler roses.

VILLA VIZCAYA
FLORIDA, U.S.A.

I remember being completely overwhelmed on first seeing the Villa Vizcaya in 1965. In the midst of the nightmare of modern Miami, this fantasy palace is an oasis of calm, beauty and inspiration. Built by John Deering in the 1920s on what was then swampland near the little resort town of Miami, the house-and-gardens mix imported fragments of Italian and Spanish architecture with new work in the local coral stone. I revisit it whenever I am in Miami.

The garden is criss-crossed by canals which bring water deep into it, shaded by giant palms. The strictness and order of the place contrasting so sharply with its air of absurd fantasy really appeals to me. A little magic in a garden is never out of place.

Facing. The Music Pavilion, like some floating relic adrift in the Florida everglades.

A ramp, between walls of Florida Keys coral stone and pink stucco, leads down to a sunk terrace garden of straight lines of box and a deliciously cooling fountain. An excellent example of simplicity of design against the exuberant carved detail of the fountain.

A wonderful parterre, almost all clipped green, enclosed by stucco and stone rustication. It has elements of European gardens of the 18th century, but a strong unity and sense of design that is absent from other creations of its time.

Everything at Villa Vizcaya arrived by water – building materials, workmen and supplies since, in the 1920s, there were no roads and no real harbour. Deering's guests would sail down with him on his yacht which moored against the striped Venetian gondola-poles between an elaborate stone barge, on which an orchestra played every evening, and the house. My favourite memory of Vizcaya was arriving there in 1976 on a friend's yacht, sailing majestically down the allée of striped poles to the house.

HESTERCOMBE
TAUNTON, ENGLAND

Lutyens's early gardens have a strong sense of design that I somehow find missing from many of his early houses, which have that rather claustrophobic, cottagey feeling that I grew up with and now loathe. Hestercombe is a good example of his early Edwardian exuberance: a water garden with a fine sense of geometry, and luxuriant, slightly abandoned planting that brings to mind the lushness and easy comfort of the life of those last years before the Great War.

What could be more romantic or delicious than these great explosions of lavender on the terrace above Lutyens's Orangery?

Facing. The intricacy and classicism of the garden are at their best in the West Water Garden, where the water flows from a stone-edged rill into a tank of waterliles. All the stone is from the local Ham Hill quarry.

As seen above and in the plan, right, from *Country Life* of 1927, Lutyens's Great Plat at Hestercombe is a perfect square laid out below the house and connecting the various parts of the garden. The planting is low and slightly rambling and loose, but all within the strict confines of the beautifully-cut stone borders.

Facing. The Pergola runs below the Great Plat. The perspective view along its length leads the eye past massed lavender. On each side other views appear between the stone column supports – back into the garden or out into the countryside.

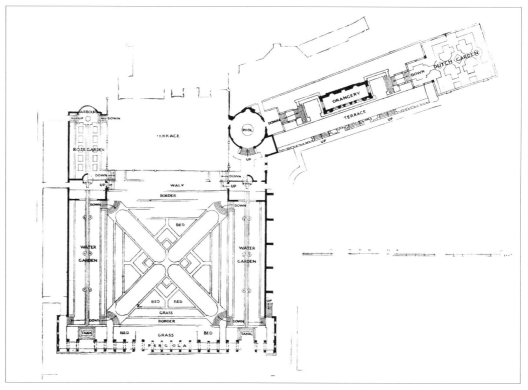

THE MOGHUL GARDEN
RASHTRAPATI BHAVAN, NEW DELHI, INDIA

I first saw what I consider to be the greatest garden of this century in the early 1960s.
It had a very profound effect on my design outlook as a whole, and there is nothing
that gives me more pleasure every time I see it.

Created by Lutyens behind his great Viceregal Palace in Delhi, finished in 1930,
it captures all that is most wonderful in the great Moghul gardens of India and
infuses them with that comfortable air of Surrey tea parties that was so much a part
of Lutyens's youth and of the Raj itself.

The house is now the home of the President of India, and the gardens are maintained
quite beautifully by the marvellously dedicated team of gardeners.

The lacy, delicate metal screen that separates the Viceroy's Court from Lutyens's magnificent avenue beyond.

An overview of the garden, with the sandstone 'fort' beyond the criss-crossing canals.

An intersection of canals with the end of the great house.

The sandstone pergola that covers the walk to the further part of the garden, with tennis courts hidden behind the screen wall to one side. Lutyens was a master of garden design and considered with great care every detail of the progression round a garden.

Water is celebrated in this driest of climates with these huge red sandstone lily-pad fountains, the water spilling off them into the canal below.

Overleaf: A dramatic view of the whole garden from the roof of the great house. The surrounding trees, which in turn are enclosed by the wide skyline, seem to emphasise the details of the garden and at the same time to accentuate its massiveness – another play of contrasts!

The Butterfly Pool was Lord Mountbatten's favourite part of the garden. The sandstone pool is surrounded with heavily-scented plantings.

Facing. Looking back at the Viceregal Palace, a simple stone path gives no clue to the complex waterworks on each side.

HIDCOTE MANOR
CHIPPING CAMPDEN, ENGLAND

At Hidcote, Laurence Johnston created in the 1930s one of the great masterpieces of garden design in England. At its centre, he formed the Stilt Garden, to my mind one of the most sublime pieces of green architecture in the world: austere, without colour, relying solely on its structure. With the contrasts of texture between grass, gravel, hornbeams, hedges and distant trees, this garden has had, and always will have, a profound influence on me.

' Hidcote is a study in the framing of views and has inspired me tremendously in this respect. In the tiny brick pavilion, Dutch in feeling, the doors are always open to frame the distant vista. I love the contrasting informality of steps and planting with the grandeur of the view.

Facing. An example of restraint. What discipline, what drama! Sharply clipped, dead-straight walls of hedge, a finely-mown lawn, natural trees at each side, all framing the distant view of the single pavilion (above).

The Stilt Garden at Hidcote relies solely on its structure for effect.

Facing: A perfectly rectangular opening cut in the yew surrounding a small pool reveals magical topiary in this small, exquisite space.

The arched form of this clipped green wall echoes the romantic roofline of the house behind, but in a modern way that I find wholly appropriate.

The stark, severe lines of the great house somehow merge into this circular box-edged lawn with a single simple urn as its centrepiece.

LONGLEAT HOUSE
WARMINSTER, ENGLAND

At Longleat is one of the best examples of Russell Page's work in this country. For the Marquess of Bath he created the perfect foil for that grandest and most fantastic of English houses, in the form of a hugely austere, plain garden of hedges and simple ornament.

The conflict between informal and formal styles of gardening which raged strongly in the 18th and 19th centuries, continues to this day. My approach to and appreciation of gardening with straight lines, rather than cultivated 'informality', is very personal. It is perhaps because so much of my working life has been spent with houses and interiors that I tend to pay particular attention to the way gardens relate to houses. Buildings tend to be based on straight lines, so I have a decided preference for straight lines near the house, constrasting with the informality of a partly man-made landscape beyond.

A splendid geometric parterre with the lush, old trees of the park behind.

As originally planted, the great parterre that Jellicoe copied from a design he found in Sir John Soane's Museum. The view is from the house towards the round bathing pool.

The enchanting round pool with water spouts was copied directly from an Italian garden.

DITCHLEY PARK
WOODSTOCK, ENGLAND

This great garden was created for Nancy Lancaster, then Mrs. Ronald Tree, in 1937 by Geoffrey Jellicoe. It was his first big job and he was steered by Nancy into creating the kind of grand, formal garden that might have been there when the house was built. Nancy made him copy parts of Kip's views of 18th century gardens. Jellicoe's wonderful parterre in front of the house has disappeared, but his pleached lime walk and background yew hedging are still to be seen.

Looking towards the house with the round pool in the foreground. When the water spouts were at their highest bathers could not be seen from the house.

LA CHEVRE D'OR

BIOT, FRANCE

This is a delightful garden, near the famous glass-blowing factory, to which I used always to go while we were lucky enough to have a house in the then relatively unspoilt south of France. The owners, Monsieur and Madame Champin, have created a marvellous garden which is full of wonderful Mediterranean textures and the subtle effects of light and shade so characteristic of this part of the world.

An open-air room with walls of clipped olive and grass makes a perfect foil for the venerable pine tree.

Facing. Terraces descend the hillside in ordered ranks of pyramids and straight lines.

THE FRICK COLLECTION
NEW YORK, U.S.A.

This small, enclosed Russell Page garden was the inspiration of Martha Symington, sister of Dr. A. Clay Frick, and a renowned gardener. It is typical of Page's detailed approach to his work in that it is designed to be seen in all seasons. Stark in winter, it is especially dramatic and lush in the summer when the lotus flowers in the pool add a subtle touch of colour.

Facing. Box-edged beds give form, while the soft planting gives the garden the 'Englishness' that is so admired.

ESSEX HOUSE

BADMINTON, ENGLAND

The late Alvilde Lees-Milne and her husband created one of the most enchanting small gardens in this country at their charming house by the gates of Badminton. I was a frequent and enthusiastic visitor and a tremendous admirer of her vision, her sense of style and her hugely knowledgeable planting. It was one of those gardens whose structure is so remarkable that they are equally enjoyable in winter as in summer, something that I have always striven for in my own garden.

I believe that design is even more important in a small garden than in a large, since space is limited and because it will be seen all the time, at a glance.

THE HUNTING LODGE
ODIHAM, ENGLAND

The distinguished interior decorator John Fowler was a very great influence in my life, and his gardening style has had a lasting effect on my own approach to garden design. He planted his lines of clipped hornbeam trees at Odiham in 1947; by the time I first saw them in the early 1950s they were already established and being cut into the rectangular lines they still have today. They were the first 'architectural' trees I saw, and I have admired them and the style ever since.

This is not a large garden, but with its clipped hedges and geometric lines it conveys a tremendous sense of space, and with its Gothick, romantic elements a sense of style and of drama, without a hint of pretentiousness. Now the property of the National Trust, it is lovingly cared for by Nicholas Haslam who lives there.

The dream-like, romantic Gothick silhouette of the Hunting Lodge is framed by strict, straight lines of green leaf, while the domed trees echo the finials of the roof line.

Facing. Looking down on the lawn from the house. The geometrical trees and obelisks against the clipped backdrop, give a marvellous sense of theatre.

One of a pair of pavilions designed by Fowler set off to the sides of the axis of the garden. They are similar in form but quite different in detail; with their curved romantic lines they make a lovely departure from the symmetry that dominates the garden.

BADMINTON HOUSE
BADMINTON, ENGLAND

After moving to the 'Big House' in 1984, the Duke and the Duchess of Beaufort created a ravishing garden. The influence is partly Russell Page, the planting the late Duchess's. It is to my mind one of the best examples of post-war garden design and planting in England.

One side of a matching pair of Russell Page gardens seen from the Duke's bedroom.

An overview of the series of small, intimate 'rooms' and walks, with the Park beyond.

A perfectly circular pool with classically-profiled bowl and fountain combines grandeur with simplicity.

HASELEY COURT
AND
THE COACH HOUSE
OXFORDSHIRE, ENGLAND

It was a great blow to me when Nancy Lancaster died in 1994. She had been a good friend for many years and a neighbour in the country, but above all, she was, for me, the greatest English gardener. She made gardens quite naturally, beautifully, stylishly and seemingly effortlessly. I loved her long, southern drawl and the dotty descriptions she would give of everything around her.

It was always a huge treat for me to be able to drive over to see her at Haseley, first in the big house and then, from 1975, in The Coach House. But she was always, whichever house she was in, in the garden.

Nancy's Stone Garden had paths of flint surrounding the cartwheel of box and lavender. Weeping mulberries stand in each corner.

Facing. Looking down from the house at the graphic simplicity of the topiary garden at Haseley with its improbable backdrop of worked fields beyond.

Two typical Nancy borders, with everything I admire in a border burgeoning forth with her loving care. The blue bench was her trademark.

Russell Page has been a great influence on so many garden designers and creators – myself and Nancy Lancaster included. This gem of a pavilion with its surrounding of mixed formal and informal planting is typical of Page's style.

Little topiary Towers of Babel in each corner of one part of the Walled Garden at Haseley Court.

The Coach House, where Nancy lived for her last twenty years. A marvellously intricate parterre of box outside this little house made it instantly as grand as her former home Ditchley Park had been in 1937.

Facing. Nancy placed this mirror in the garden to 'lengthen' the view and create a sense of space.

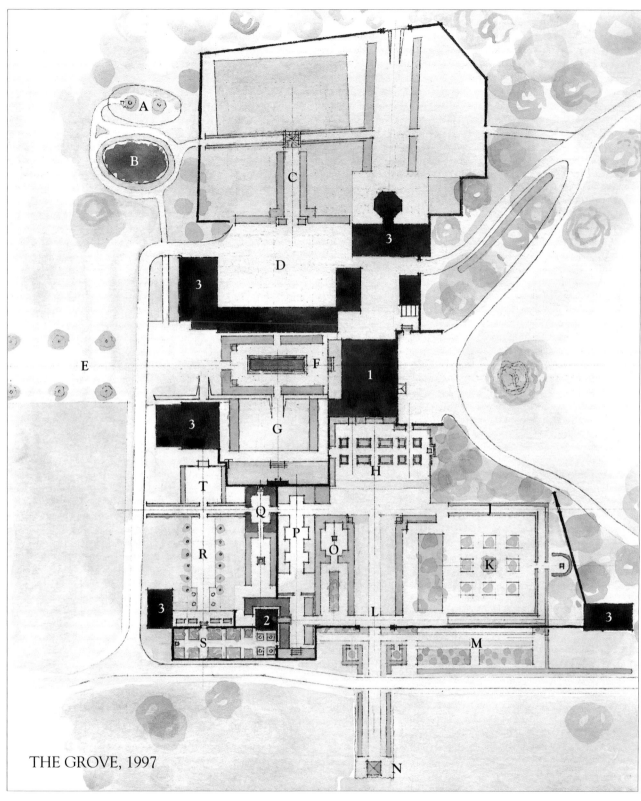

THE GROVE, 1997

1: The House
2: Pavilion
3: Outbuildings
A: Mount
B: Pond
C: Lime allée and rustic arbour walled garden

D: Stable yard
E: Chestnut avenue
F: Swimming pool with clipped chestnuts
G: Upper lawn with pleached limes and terrace
H: Drawing room parterre

J: Tunnel
K: Magnolia Garden
L: Clairvoyée and stilt trees
M: Mrs. Ashley's Garden
N: Hornbeam 'tent'
O: Statue Garden
P: Pot Garden

Q: Red Garden
R: Catalpa Walk
S: Secret Garden
T: Gothic Summerhouse

THE GROVE
BECOMING A GARDENER

It was not until 1980, when we sold Britwell Salome, and moved to this much smaller house, that I started garden designing in earnest. The Grove is essentially a farmhouse with a Regency drawing room added on. The garden I found here was haphazard and rambling, enclosed everywhere by walls and black barns which blocked the views of the country around. With the exception of some very good trees nearby and some fine stone and brick walls, I was left with an open canvas to work on. I made what is now, eighteen years later, an unusual and mature garden.

Immediately I yearned for some of the feeling of space and openness that we had enjoyed at Britwell, with its commanding views. I quickly realised that on this very flat piece of land, on which the house lies low, I had to create vistas. Working from the inside of the house, from the views out of the principle rooms, I started to devise a plan.

My first act was to open the views from drawing and dining rooms, framing the resulting clairvoyées with lines of trees, chestnuts for the west-facing dining room, quick-growing hornbeams for the drawing room. The chestnuts I underplanted with chestnut hedges, the only ones I know of. They surround the black-painted pool which leads the eye to the Spanish chestnut avenue beyond and thence to the ride that I cut through a distant belt of trees to terminate this vista.

From the drawing room, beyond the gated clairvoyée, the focal point is a green 'tent' of clipped hornbeam on a metal frame, in the centre of two L-shaped stilt hornbeam walls with hornbeam hedges below them. Through the gates, to one side lies the cutting rose garden with two large beds of my favourite cutting roses. With their backs to the south wall are lined up twenty Chinese and Japanese tree peonies in pots.

In 1990, as a sixtieth birthday present, my wife sweetly gave me a pavilion of my own design and this became the focus of a whole new area of the garden, an area of smaller spaces which formed a circuit through which many like-minded people have toured my garden, something I have found very rewarding and flattering. The canal around three sides of the pavilion was formed in 1994. Over its drawbridge is the Secret Garden filled with old roses, peonies, foxgloves, lilies, hostas and salvia.

Beyond this lies a lime walk, an allée of catalpa trees and the Red Room of copper beech stilt trees and hedges framing four obelisks, covered in 'Danse du Feu' rose, and one of several water features, a limestone jar with water spilling over gently into a basin below. I have always loved the sound of running water which, even in chilly England, reminds me of the luxuriant atmosphere of Provençal summers long ago.

My garden, like so much of my work, very quickly started to be published, and seen and talked about. Friends asked advice for their own gardens; the gardens around clients' houses needed thought; and so I began a new career in garden design, all based on my experience in Oxfordshire.

Looking out from the front of the house on a misty summer's morning, a lone, majestic ilex tree with the distant outline of the Chiltern hills beyond.

The Gothick arch in the Chinese Chippendale porch leads into the garden.

Facing. I added the Chinese Chippendale porch to the front door when we moved to The Grove, as a late completion of the Regency transformation of this simple farmhouse into a pretty dower house. At first I placed tubs with standard gooseberry bushes to either side, later replaced by the pair of bronze leopards which stand on simple cement block bases.

The drawing room vista as it was first laid out. Before the hornbeam 'tent' was made, I continued the mown central path towards the fields, with wild, long grass to either side. I sketched on to a photograph of the just-mown lawn, just-planted hornbeams and the urns an impression of how the garden would be when mature. The sketch (below) lived behind the drawing room curtains for years, and I would gaze at it to calm my impatient longing for my creation to be complete.

Right. Looking back from within the hornbeam 'tent' to the house, showing how simple the view looks in reverse, with the urns hidden.

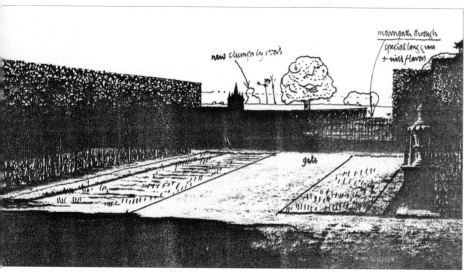

The drawing room, added to the house around 1820, is much grander than the other rooms and demanded a suitably grand prospect from its large Regency window framed by my rather elaborate pink cotton curtains. The view is perfectly symmetrical, with everything, including the clairvoyée opening in the far wall, centred precisely on the window. I planted strict lines of quick-growing hornbeam trees with hedges slightly behind, in the manner of the Marly of Louis XIV. In the recessed angles of these stand a pair of rather grand 18th century statuary urns brought from our old house, which are thus concealed by the trees when looking back at the house, against which they would look exaggerated and pompous.

Outside, the completed view after eighteen years' work. The hornbeams are perfectly mature and full, and closely clipped into architectural walls of green; in the foreground is my new box parterre, in the distance the hornbeam 'tent' framed by further hornbeam hedges.

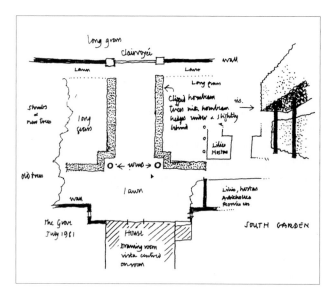

A sketch plan of the South Garden showing the first elements which I added when we arrived: the urns, the lines of hornbeam trees and hedges, the pierced 'clairvoyée' in the far wall.

As cappings to the new piers of the clairvoyée in the old wall, I designed these very simple pinnacles in painted plywood, a good foil to the elaborate carved stone urns. Beyond, an old cottage with fretwork gable against some of the magnificent old trees that surround us.

Facing. The statue of Flora, like the urns, we brought with us from our old house. To prevent her looking pretentious or out of place in this small garden, I placed her very low on a plain cement base, against an existing background of rambling yew and trees.

The west face of the house is of chalk cut on the estate, whose soft ivory colour is wonderful in summer with my roses ('Lady Hillingdon' among them) climbing against it. While I love climbers to ramble and sprawl with romantic abundance, I do not like to see them from inside the house, where they might disturb the interior design. I added the Gothick windows to the ground floor, with Gothick French windows from the dining room to the terrace, which is paved with old York stone around two beds planted with lavender, box, nicotiana and feverfew.

Facing. I boldly placed my 8 feet wide by 38 feet long swimming pool 40 feet from my dining room window and made it the central focal point of that particular side of my garden. Painted black it does not in any way look like a heated, filtered pool; it looks like a formal piece of water. The surround is of inexpensive paving slabs bordered by large pebbles set in cement. The pool reflects the house's dramatic deep-gabled silhouette.

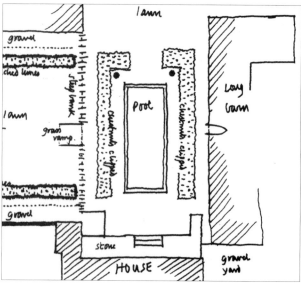

I composed the view from the dining room from within, placing pool on axis and enclosed by clipped chestnuts, with a chestnut avenue beyond leading the eye to the horizon, where a small opening cut through an old belt of trees suggests a vista of enormous distance. My original French windows had obscured the centre of this view and I eventually replaced them with this 'Hindoo-Gothick' sash window with hinged apron below.

Facing. An overview from the top of the house reveals how the very grand vista is in fact set in Oxfordshire farmland, with fields, barns and random clumps of old trees all around.

My sixtieth birthday present, a
crenellated pavilion on the foundations
of an old bothy next to my Secret
Garden. The ogee Gothick windows are
topped with carved stone finials that I
had kept for years before finding this use
for them.

Facing the pavilion, in front of the stilt
hornbeam trees and hedges, I placed
artichokes in plastic pots within
architecturally-clipped blocks of
hawthorn. I find this very unusual use of
hawthorn interesting, not least because
it is, to my knowledge, unique. I am
always trying to avoid established habits
and clichés, and to break the mould by
providing new answers to old problems.

Pierced doorways, whatever the style, add enormous interest to a garden when carefully integrated with their surroundings. This arched gateway leads into the Secret Garden and frames the carefully positioned urn completing the vista. In planning The Grove garden I sometimes found myself becoming over-preoccupied with straight lines, so I allowed the element of human error to creep in to the most formal of approaches. This gives a certain warmth to what could otherwise be too austere.

The Secret Garden beside the pavilion. Its small size and surrounding walls make the sight and smell of this garden almost overpowering in summer, with poppies, tree peonies, roses, lilies and foxgloves jostling each other for one's attention.

I surrounded the pavilion on two sides with water, a shallow moat covered in waterlilies in the summer. The drawbridge causes great amusement. I raise it from within by a hand-cranked mechanism when I desire isolation from the world. The circular panel contains knapped flints picked from the fields around.

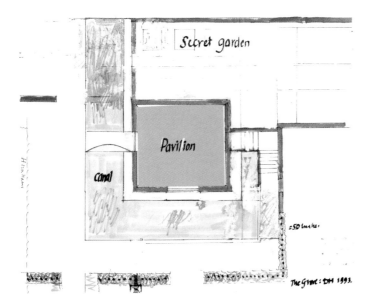

My drawing of the area around the pavilion with the Secret Garden at the top; the Red Garden is sited at the bottom.

Position is everything in garden design. On the axis of the Red Garden with the pavilion I placed this limestone fountain in which the water falls from the urn into a pool in the base.

Above and facing above. The Pot Garden. Framed by the pavilion and by a line of pleached hornbeams, I placed on squares of gravel similar groups of varied containers, all painted green, some octagonal, some square, some Versailles planters. All are, in fact, bottomless, everything being planted directly into the ground below. This reduces the maintenance needed both for the plants, which need less water, and for the containers, which go into a barn for the winter. The plants are mostly box, with some crambe, which I love for its architectural quality. The octagonal forms hold sedum, which they keep tightly controlled.

A doorway combining the contrasted shapes of arch and turret. Apertures are extremely important in any garden design. A tall, narrow gap between hedges, an opening in a wall, the way through from one part of a garden to another lends excitement and drama to the atmosphere.

Containers of good proportion can add greatly to the character of gardens large and small. I designed this variation on a Versailles tub for my own house. Here I am firming in a giant sunflower. I also dig, fork, hoe, prune, plant and sow.

Above and facing. Through the centre of the old walled garden, I made a simple tunnel of wire netting connecting two existing doorways, all planted with climbing 'American Pillar' roses. At right angles to this, an allée of pleached limes approaches from the stable yard. Where the two meet, I formed a rustic arbour of stumpwork. Behind the limes are large rhubarb plants whose leaves I like to arrange with flowers.

Stumpwork is the elaborate and decorative arrangement of stumps of wood or tree roots to give a rustic effect. It can be used in all sorts of imaginative ways in a garden – for arches, pavilions, gates, borders, and so on.

Working in the garden 1994. I do not think anyone who is not a working gardener can have a really good garden.

Away from the garden, beyond the barns, I made a small pond which, in summer, becomes a mass of huge
water-loving plants and a haven for dragonflies. Here I have gunnera, heracleum and Japanese dogwood.
Facing, the pond in 1988; and above, ten years later.

I am fortunate enough not only to live in the midst of beautiful country, but also to own just enough of it to be able to control the look of the landscape that surrounds and is seen from my garden. I do not allow the growing of that offensively fluorescent yellow rape, instead planting flax across our land which turns the whole landscape a delicate powder blue for two weeks in the early summer. I have also planted many thousands of trees, great belts of them that will one day replace lovely old trees such as this.

Some years ago I found an old trailer wheelbase, on to which I constructed a sharply tapered plywood pyramid with a tiny quatrefoil window and a door just big enough for my grandchildren to enter. This I have towed to whichever position catches my fancy. Here it is blocking the offensive sight of a bright orange tiled roof in a neighbouring village which I could otherwise see from my desk.

GARDENS I ADMIRE

One of my great pleasures is to travel and discover new friends with a similar passion for their gardens in far-flung corners of the globe. And I am just as happy to drive over to someone in the next county and see how their roses are coming on.

I was brought up in the world of gardening and my ideas have come from what I have seen in other people's gardens – in Australia, India, America and South Africa as well as in Europe.

Planning and planting in a stylish way make up good garden design. It is no use having small groups of plants mixed up together; you must be very bold in your planting. If you have old-fashioned roses, have a lot of them, the massing of plants is very important. If you have a formal rose bed make sure that all the roses are the same colour, or at least are planted in blocks of colour.

Design is the essence of a good garden. Gardens should be like houses and have rooms; spaces should be contained by hedges, wall, fences or rows of trees.

A letter I wrote to a client in England in February 1990 sums up many of my thoughts and feelings about the sort of gardens I admire:

I am writing in the air between Johannesburg and Capetown. I thought I would take the opportunity to describe your garden as I see it in late June 1991. I have borne in mind that there will not be a full-time gardener so that there will not be all that suburban mown grass and thousands of crevices between cracked bricks – perfectly hideous to weed!

There will be no flower garden as such, no rose garden and no herbaceous borders but there will be twelve garden rooms, some of which will be furnished with accents of colour provided by old roses, new English roses and cutting roses such as 'Peace', 'Fragrant Cloud', 'Etoile de Hollande' and 'New Dawn'. Other 'rooms' will be devoted to tree peonies, fuchsias, buddleias and shrubs to provide autumn colour. In June you will be the possessor of a scented garden: honeysuckle, choisya, roses, jasmine, buddleia, virburnum, philadelphus, lavender.

The lines of chestnut, lime or hornbeam will be looking less like private school people, and the grass on the recently levelled lawn will hopefully look like a Regency striped wallpaper. The terrace gravel will scrunch underfoot whilst the eye will feast on big squares of lavender and box and on the climbing roses 'Caroline Testout', 'Lady Waterlow' (so *pushing*), 'Lady Hillingdon' (always *actively* in bloom), and 'Constance Spry'. They are old beauties and I am afraid, like a lot of old ladies, somewhat demanding of one's attention.

I have many garden pals whose work I admire hugely, and it has been a treat to put together photographs of some of my favourites.

Facing. Seen from an upper window of the house, Jane's White Garden at its absolute peak, in the fullness of early summer, white roses bursting forth on every side, the path meandering subtly through the middle. In the joints of the stone paving Jane planted small surprises to peep out at one; the beds to either side are full to bursting with hostas and other old friends.

UNDERWOOD HALL

NEWMARKET, ENGLAND

My very great friend Jane, Lady Adeane, whose tragic death robbed me of many shared joys, among them a wicked sense of humour and an all-consuming passion for gardens, made a wonderful garden at the house where she lived with my wife's cousin Noel Cunningham-Reid. Her gardening had a softness and romance that I enjoyed hugely, contrasting as it did with my own more masculine world of straight lines and hard edges. I made various elaborate plans for the garden including the cutting of vistas through distant woods, not all of which were executed. We always kept up a vigorous correspondence on all aspects of our outdoor life, one that I miss very greatly.

BARNARDS
SIBLE HEDINGHAM, ENGLAND

In only five years my friends Dorothy and Leonard Ratcliffe created this wonderful garden, not far from Coggeshall where I grew up. I admire much of the garden for its sureness and its strong sense of design, just as I admire its splendidly stubborn creator who, when told by me to cut down an asymmetrically placed pear tree, refused, instead carefully weaving it into her new garden plan.

A very unusual allée, or 'forthright' as the Elizabethans would have said, of Irish junipers rising from burgeoning clumps of 'Imperial Gem' lavender leads to a pergola of honeysuckle *Lonicera americana*.

Facing. Dorothy Ratcliffe's 'Mondrian' garden, named for its geometric design, suggested by her sculptor daughter. I find the crisp regularity of it, with its dramatic central feature of pleached hawthorns and pachysandra, immensely self-assured and sophisticated in the midst of the Essex countryside of my own childhood. Stone balls surround the central feature with its radiating patterns of inlaid brick.

THE MANOR HOUSE
BLEDLOW, ENGLAND

Lord and Lady Carrington, together with the landscape architect Robert Adams, started to make the garden some thirty years ago. At that time the house was surrounded by farmyard, paddocks and shrubbery, but with clever planning and planting and immense imagination the garden has evolved into charming individual areas, each with its own characteristics.

The armillary sphere with its circular hoops is perfectly placed in the centre of the Topiary Garden to complement the precise clipping.

Facing. The Manor House, Bledlow. Some years ago, at the entrance to the Sculpture Garden, the Carringtons created a series of lily ponds crossed by a brick bridge.

In the old walled garden, away from the house, Peter Saunders made a new tennis court, swimming pool and this lovely small garden, surrounded by a well-clipped yew hedge, with little stone sculptures and a romantic profusion of roses.

Peter Coats designed several garden seats for the house, among them this enchanting one in white-painted wood, wrapping around a tree, copied from an early 18th century example.

Facing. Wyatt's south front of 1820 with the ancient wisterias. His new, large Regency window replaced the original front door. The sundial and the stone-edged beds are the best kind of Victorian gardening, while the Cotswold stone walls are wonderfully local in character and place the house so precisely in the geography of English gardens.

EASTON GREY
MALMESBURY, ENGLAND

This lovely mid-18th century house was transformed in 1820 by Wyatt, who 'turned the house around', adding a new entrance portico to one side and large Regency windows to the original entrance front. The windows face south over the river Avon, and on to a new garden which is a great example of good, restrained Victorian layout. It has the pretty but relaxed formality of stone-edged beds and sundials, but without the strident colouring or excess of curvature. The house is now blessed with two 100-year old wisterias, one Japanese, the other Chinese, all over the front, and with the kind of mature, splendid cedars and other trees that one only finds on an old English estate.

I knew the house extremely well some 25 years ago when I worked there for Mr. and Mrs. Peter Saunders, for whom I created two of the most glamorous and sophisticated bathrooms anywhere. The late Peter Coats was a great friend of theirs (and ours) and made various contributions to the garden at Easton Grey.

BARNSLEY HOUSE
CIRENCESTER, ENGLAND

The distinguished plantswoman Rosemary Verey designed this garden with deliberation and imagination, exploring many styles and influences. Within the four-acre garden there are vistas, features and paths, a decorative potager, a laburnum walk and a knot garden based on a 16th century embroidery pattern. To my mind its success lies in strong contrasts of style, with the symmetry of disciplined design and close clipping softened by rich and unusual planting.

The 17th century Doric temple looks over an informally planted pool.

Facing. The vista down the shaded laburnum walk. The cobbled path is bordered by hostas and flowering alliums.

HATFIELD HOUSE

HATFIELD, ENGLAND

At Hatfield that enormously talented and resourceful gardener Lady Salisbury made a herb garden in front of the Old Palace. The building, of around 1490, was used as a royal nursery (for children, not plants) by Henry VIII; young Princess Elizabeth was held captive there during her sister's reign, and the thought of the future Queen walking in the garden inspired Lady Salisbury's marvellously authentic reconstruction.

The plants are all known to have been used in the 16th and early 17th centuries,

including sweet rocket, day lilies, purple *Gladiolus byzantinus* and many old roses together with herbs; all within intricate knots of box hedging. The first great English gardener worked at Hatfield: John Tradescant collected plants for the first Earl of Salisbury, and his fascination with new and varied species is reflected in this garden. In the end, however, it is entirely the creation of Lady Salisbury, who has also made, at Cranborne in Dorset, what must be the pinnacle of perfection in English gardening.

A fountain centrepiece in a cool green 'garden room' in another part of the garden at Hatfield.

Facing. Lady Salisbury's reconstructed herb garden uses plants grown in the 16th and 17th centuries.

THE RECTORY
OXFORDSHIRE, ENGLAND

Christopher Gibbs lives not far from me in the country, in a lovely old house built by his ancestors. Around it he has made the most wonderful garden, full of his peculiarly English vision of grand scale and diverting whims, using both existing features and recent introductions. I love to drive over and see what he is up to, since there is always some new and unlikely arrival in his bit of England.

A slightly forlorn-looking cow, which originally graced a dairy in Dublin, is framed against a massive boulder shape in clipped yew, planted in the 1840s.

Facing. The delightfully shady Lime Walk leads to a vast pot of typically Gibbsian proportions. A true master of scale.

THE OLD RECTORY
SUDBOROUGH, ENGLAND

Over the last fifteen years Mr. and Mrs. Anthony Huntington have created from absolutely nothing this lovely garden within old walls of stone and brick. I love its romance, the secrecy of the hidden potager, its atmosphere of the mediaeval. It has something of the feeling of an early monastery garden or one glimpsed through the open window in a Dutch Renaissance portrait, with tidy compart-ments of herbs and flowers divided by brick paths and water.

The door into the walled potager, where a pergola carries 'Violette' roses over the tiled path.

Facing. The Huntingtons designed this slightly Chinese Chippendale bridge themselves. Its drab green colour is perfect for the location.

THE OLD SCHOOL HOUSE
LANGFORD, ENGLAND

Sir Hardy Amies came to this house some 25 years ago and has created a magical, lovely garden. It is particularly designed to be looked down upon from the first floor of the house, which gives it a strong, geometric character that greatly appeals to me. The exuberant, romantic planting within strict borders of sharply clipped box is very much to my own taste. The old roses, honeysuckle, foxgloves, clematis and nicotiana are all great favourites of my own, but set against a very local Cotswold stone background which differs from my own context of brick, chalk and flint.

The circular, Cotswold tiled summerhouse is so much in the local vernacular, while the ball-topped-and-footed stone obelisks are so particularly the owner's. I relish the contrast of strict formal planning and romantic, lush planting, here seen in the height of a lovely English summer.

BUCKINGHAM PALACE
LONDON, ENGLAND

There is nothing I loathe more than really unimaginative, fussy herbaceous borders bristling with colour of every kind, laid out without the slightest idea of design or form. They take me straight back to the Essex gardens of my childhood. On occasion, however, such as here in Her Majesty The Queen's garden at Buckingham Palace, scene of so many garden parties, the sheer scale and quality of the planting has such a tremendous effect that the result is quite breathtaking.

The garden contains all the subtle ingredients that go to make a good herbaceous border: great clumps of plants in a variety of colour, texture and height, all carefully considered before being perfectly positioned.

CRICHEL
DORSET, ENGLAND

The Hon. Mrs. Marten, over a number of years, has created at Crichel a wonderful garden in the old walled vegetable garden of her house. The garden is an exercise of great restraint and simplicity, a play of straight lines and formal elements enclosed within the old brick walls, its clean geometry contrasting with the picturesque planting of the 18th century park outside.

The lime walk was planted nearly thirty years ago and the sureness of hand and mastery of scale with which it was done are now supremely evident.

Facing. Two views of the walled garden at Crichel: the rose bower with radiating paths; and the parallel lines of box hedges.

PARSON'S PIECE

OXFORDSHIRE, ENGLAND

My daughter Edwina lives next to us in the country in a chalk barn that she and her husband, Jeremy Brudenell, have converted in a sensitive and interesting way into a house. Jeremy, who has a thriving gardening business and a nursery nearby, has created, to one side of the house, this small garden with a crisp geometry that contrasts splendidly with the rolling fields beyond. Divided by gravel paths, it has four wooden pyramids with climbing roses in beds surrounded by box. At the centre is a good scale terracotta pot on a brick base.

RAINTHORPE HALL
NEAR NORWICH, ENGLAND

I love the almost extravagant simplicity of this extraordinary garden. The bold ornamental quality of the parterre, the rambling old roses against brick, and the romantic silhouette of the roofline all summon an image of those long-lost English gardens swept away by Brown and Repton.

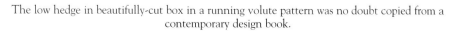

The low hedge in beautifully-cut box in a running volute pattern was no doubt copied from a contemporary design book.

Delicate ironwork gates give a tantalising view towards the house.

Spirited Gothic trellis walls enclose this very dramatic garden of square beds around an old sundial. The slightly forced formality of the garden contrasts beautifully with the naturalism of the off-centre tree beyond.

View through a Gothic-inspired trellis arch towards the conservatory and house.

Facing. John Stefanidis designed the new conservatory very much in sympathy with the house. It looks down on Arabella Lennox-Boyd's playful geometric garden arranged around a hexagonal lead cistern, with a covered bench in each corner.

FORT BELVEDERE
WINDSOR, ENGLAND

This enchanting house within the demesne of Windsor Castle was, of course, famous as the Prince of Wales's country house before the Second World War.

More recently a wonderful garden has been created there with great vision by Mrs. Galen Weston with help from Arabella Lennox-Boyd, Rosemary Verey and John Stefanidis, who also redecorated the house.

The marvellously romantic, battlemented castle backdrop has found a perfect foil in the rather strict geometry of the new garden.

A pool alive with waterlilies and a handsome Chinese Chippendale seat framed by topiary cones act as the focus for the house.

From field to garden, through fence, lawn, trees, and soft, old brickwork covered with roses.

Facing. A direct statement in simple topiary, enclosed by hedges and walls.

ROFFORD MANOR

NEAR OXFORD, ENGLAND

At a beautiful and secluded house near mine in the country, the owners have made a lovely, simple garden within and around the old walls. A wonderful English country garden atmosphere comes with the measured transition from the mellowed brickwork over the lawn to the fields beyond.

In the courtyard, rather French-feeling trees with box 'slippers' on their feet.

Facing. A garden vista at Rofford Manor – looking through an ivied arch to formal and informal arrangements of plants.

ASHTON WOLD

ASHTON, ENGLAND

The distinguished zoologist and botanist Dr. Miriam Rothschild has created at her home one of the most magical and extraordinary gardens I have ever seen. Everywhere you turn is a view out of some Victorian fairy painting, with great sweeping drifts of wild flowers scattered beneath mature trees. This is truly a paradise. I love the dream-like quality of the place, the abandoned naturalism of it, the complete lack of any sort of pretentiousness.

The garden is a veritable nature reserve with wild flowers, 'weeds' and cultivated plants flourishing cheek by jowl. In early summer cow parsley makes a wonderfully delicate backcloth for laburnum and parrot tulips, and is prolific under trees. The adjoining wild flower fields are full of birds, butterflies and insects, giving a romantic 'wilderness' quality to the whole garden.

EASTON NESTON
TOWCESTER, ENGLAND

On the West Front of this marvellous Hawksmoor house, Lord Hesketh's head gardener in the 1920s made a new garden around an existing lead figure, with water, topiary and stone statues bought at the great house sale at neighbouring Stowe.

Looking from the house, to the new water which is framed by great, curving wings of yew punctuated by fine statues. I love the simplicity of the yew discs and the great spiral volutes of golden box to each side, so very Baroque.

LE CLOS FIORENTINA
CAP FERRAT, FRANCE

I first knew this as part of Rory Cameron's garden when he lived in such colossal style at La Fiorentina, and then when he had moved into Le Clos and really worked on the garden in the 1970s. I then decorated the house for Sao Schlumberger and used to bring my children over to swim, from our own house by the harbour at St. Jean, while I worked. Since Hubert de Givenchy bought the house, the garden has had a real renaissance, thanks to his infallible sense of style and his extraordinary eye brought to bear on every corner of this enchanted place. It is now, I would say, by far the best garden in the South of France.

The dining terrace, scene of many a protracted lunch-party, shaded by a wonderful vine, which looks across at Beaulieu and the Alpes Maritimes. Sadly the very handsome furniture I designed for the terrace 20 years ago is long gone.

I adore the romance of this great drift of lavender with cypresses behind.

Tree trunks painted white in that lovely Provençal manner take me back to long, hot summers of 50 years ago.

Facing. At the top of this terraced garden at Le Clos Fiorentina, a shady pergola with weeping vines and a cool stone wall.

LE PETIT FONTANILLE

ST. ETIENNE DU GRES, FRANCE

The Hon. Anne Cox Chambers, American Ambassador to Brussels during the Carter Presidency, lives between Atlanta and Provence. At this house near Avignon she has a remarkable garden originally laid out some 18 years ago by Peter Coats and later added to by Rory Cameron and others. The garden is large and complex, including a working *jardin potager* which provides the most delicious local food. I have always loved this part of the world and to see someone live there today in such great style is a rare delight.

On one edge of the long terrace at Le Petit Fontanille lies this small herb garden of concentric beds edged by low box hedges interspersed with gravel paths. The railings and gates are of weathered teak; the metal obelisk frames support roses and runner beans. In the fenced enclosure beyond is the cutting flower garden.

Facing. A simple path of stone slabs set into the lawn with a backdrop of magnificent cypresses.

CHEMIN DU MOULIN
OPIO, FRANCE

When I first started in business in the late 1950s, it was as Hicks & Parr. Tom Parr went on to take Colefax & Fowler and transform it from John Fowler's little office and shop into a major international business. In 1984 he bought a house in the South of France and over the last 14 years has made the most wonderful and atmospheric garden.

I find it extremely stylish that the long terrace is treated rather like a long gallery in an English country house, furnished with beautifully clipped box tables and sofa, and vases arranged against the wall, above which (left) is this enchanting little path between lavender and cypresses.

Facing. Great drifts of lavender burgeon forth on either side of the gravel path that runs beneath the charmingly simple metal-framed pergola covered in all of Tom's favourite roses, among them 'Penelope'.

At Chemin du Moulin the strict geometry of the ruthlessly clipped topiary masses contrasts brilliantly with the loose natural forms of the old trees.

The view from the terrace is sublime, but I really admire the sure touch of the glazed vase on its simple brick base, set in a carpet of balls of pittosporum 'Le Nain'. This would be every bit as successful, to my mind, in a tiny city backyard as it is here with the magnificent landscape beyond.

Facing. At Chemin du Moulin a circular pool, edged in local stone, is luxuriously sprouting waterlilies in Tom Parr's garden. Two old terracotta pots hold blue plumbago; the statue of Spring is a good 18th century one.

PALAIS SETEIZ
SINTRA, PORTUGAL

This lovely old palace in the historic centre of northern Portugal is now an hotel but has lost little of the charm and elegance that it had when I visited it with Madame Ghani while planning her Vila Verde in the Algarve.

The utter simplicity of this geometrical play on spheres and rectangular solids cut in topiary has, for me, lasting appeal. It is another example of small-scale, stylish gardening that will always be successful, regardless of the location.

VILA BRAMAO
ALGARVE, PORTUGAL

While planning the garden at Vila Verde in Portugal, I returned again and again for inspiration to my old friend Dom Luiz Bramao who created, at his wonderful villa the most delightful, neat, ordered and civilised garden in Southern Portugal. Entirely of box, surrounded by his fascinating collection of classical fragments and objects, it is an oasis of calm and culture. To protect against the fierce heat of the Portuguese summer with its hot African winds, Dom Luiz devised an ingenious net ceiling which can be stretched rather picturesquely above the garden.

FOXHALL ROAD

WASHINGTON D.C., U.S.A.

Mrs. William McCormick Blair, Jr., has at her house in Washington this hugely stylish little courtyard garden outside the dining room. The space, framed by the open arcade with its Jeffersonian Chippendale balustrade, was first laid out by Russell Page and later altered by Michael Bartlett. There are several different miniature box hedges, varieties developed by the late Mr. Holman, including 'Green Cushion' which is also used at the White House.

In the centre is an old and treasured verdigris metal basket which Mrs. Blair found many years ago in the basement of Mallett at Bourdon House. This is planted differently every year to give the effect of a basket of mixed flowers in a house, often with a lot of herbs, mint, catnip and blue and white flowers.

OLD WESTBURY

LONG ISLAND, U.S.A.

Old Westbury was built as the country house of John Phipps of New York City in the first decade of the 20th century and stands today as a poignant reminder of that pre-war era of confidence and luxury. The garden, which remains in extraordinarily perfect condition, has an exuberance and vitality in its heady planting that is framed by the restrained and elegant architecture surrounding it. I have long admired the Walled Garden, a little way from the house itself, with its Lotus Pool and handsome pergolas.

The Lotus Pool at Old Westbury stands at the far end of the Walled Garden, framed by the exedra form of the long pergola. This green-painted wood structure is redolent of the *fin de siècle* garden.

Looking across the Lotus Pool at the high Edwardian-style stone balustrade and pergola.

Facing. From within the pergola, the full expanse of the Walled Garden at Old Westbury stretches out beyond the Lotus Pool in the foreground. The path leads up to the gate entrance; the house itself is away to the right, hidden in the trees.

FIRST NECK LANE

LONG ISLAND, U.S.A.

As a young man, Mark Hampton worked for me in London and then was my American associate before going on to make his own hugely successful career in which he decorated everything that mattered from the White House down. We have remained close through the years and make periodic visits of appraisal to each other's gardens, in which admiration is mixed with friendly criticism and a great deal of laughter. The garden in Southampton, Long Island, that Mark and his wife Duane have created is wonderfully fresh and simple, redolent of the spirit of early American life.

The pergola framing the view of the house is approached along a smooth grass path, bordered by box and backed by blossom trees.

Facing. The path to the white obelisk at First Neck Lane is bordered with lilies, hostas and mint. Behind the obelisk, a trellis is covered with scrambling morning glory.

The white picket fence around the swimming pool has 'New Dawn' roses climbing over and blooming spectacularly in mid-June, the gates opening on to a small garden.

Facing above. A section of the small front garden at First Neck Lane which is divided into four segments. Bordered in low boxwood, and with eight flowering crab apple trees, the garden includes pink and white peonies, roses of all sorts, foxgloves, violets, astilbe, and blue and white hydrangeas.

Facing below. A bench in the Hampton's garden covered with a white clematis vine that blooms profusely at the end of the summer.

BASS GARDEN
FORT WORTH, U.S.A.

One of Russell Page's last jobs was this garden for Anne Bass at her extraordinary modern house in Texas, designed in 1981. Page was not an admirer of architect Paul Rudolph's house, but to my mind the juxtaposition of this modern essay in white steel with the crisp green geometry of the Page garden and the imaginative placing of sculpture in the swimming pool (left) makes this one of the most exciting gardens I have ever seen.

Russell Page's allée of pleached live oak trees has a hard, sculptural quality perfectly in sympathy with Paul Rudolph's angular modernist house. Floating planes of white steel are framed by the floating block of green leaves.

Facing. Sunk below the house and the oak allée is this geometric play of square beds edged in box. It is approached by stone steps from the house and leading in turn to the rectangular lily pool.

MAYFAIR
LONG ISLAND, U.S.A.

Mrs. Betty Sherrill of the great New York decorating firm McMillen, Inc., has made a very unusual and rather magical garden in Southampton, Long Island, where she annually hosts a splendid Daffodil Lunch when thousands of bulbs are in bloom.

I am not keen on the commoner yellow daffodils, those great big 'King Alfreds' that are so invasive in the English spring. Indeed I try to stop them on my own land, and take great pleasure in driving through the larger clumps of them in my Range Rover. Here, however, in these mixed daffodils and narcissi, there is something so spectacular, so truly romantic, like a pot of gold in a fairy tale.

FILOLI

SAN FRANCISCO, U.S.A.

What appeals to me about the elegant Lurline B. Roth Gardens in the 654-acre estate of Filoli, are the separate areas which lead so effortlessly one to another, yet each maintaining its individuality. From the central walled garden with its symmetrical planting of pink and silver, a path leads to the cool green woodland garden, another to the amazing Chartres Cathedral Window Garden, where the outlines of miniature box represent the leading and the red and vermilion planting the glazing of one of the cathedral's stained glass windows.

The design of the Knot Garden at Filoli is made up of interlocking patterns of herbs and other plants. The intricate clumping together of contrasting textures and colours involves hard work, but creates marvellous effects.

The symmetry of the planting in the sunken garden is emphasised by the pruned trees around. In the background, over the top of the pool pavilion, a honey locust is at its most splendid.

Facing. Filoli is full of exquisitely pruned and shaped olive trees, like these cut in the form of a massive drum.

The terrace outside the dining room at 19 Star Island was made by Peter Coats with a simple paved stone floor to his design, cast stone urns on pedestals containing agave set against a tightly-clipped, tall hedge of podocarpus that creates a marvellous sense of perspective. Beyond is a 19th century Italian Bacchus.

19 STAR ISLAND
MIAMI, FLORIDA, U.S.A.

I decorated the new house of prominent Miami lawyer Daniel S. Paul in 1970. It was sited in a magical position on one of the string of islands next to Miami Beach. Dan became a great friend of all our family and the project continued for many years: I have now finished his new house on another island. My old friend Peter Coats designed the garden for him in 1980, creating small enclosed spaces around the house that were designed to show best at night when artificially lit. These pictures show just that.

The pool had tremendous style and a restrained chic not often seen in gaudy Miami. Between the stone obelisks is a 1930s white-painted wood bench that Peter Coats insisted on re-using, despite his client wanting to throw it out. Beyond is a hugely dramatic view of Biscayne Bay.

WHITE WOOD
CAPTAIN'S NECK, SOUTHAMPTON, U.S.A.

Mrs. John Mortimer is a great gardener and has been gardening editor of several American magazines. At her own house in the country she made this wonderful cottage garden with a pretty picket gate leading to a box hedge-lined path and a pergola beyond covered with rambling climber roses. This is a great example of simple, restrained gardening in the old American tradition.

GUNSTON HALL
VIRGINIA, U.S.A.

Gunston Hall is best known for its exquisitely carved interiors, the work of an Oxfordshire man, William Buckland, who worked on the house until 1759. The lovely garden behind the house was planted shortly thereafter and is a rare American survival from the age of true certainty of design and clarity of line. The round porch on the garden front of the house, with its cusped arches, has the effect of a garden pavilion above the topiary, its somewhat Chinese lines echoed in the fretwork bench back.

GIN LANE
LONG ISLAND, U.S.A.

Mr. and Mrs. Milton Petrie, the great benefactors of the arts who gave the splendid sculpture court to the Metropolitan Museum of Art in New York, made this garden with a rigorous simplicity very much in my own taste. Plain brick paving between sharply-clipped box hedges with standards leads past a sundial to a broad lawn; here a majestic allée of fruit trees frames a distant gazebo with a tented Chinese roof.

TEMPLETON
LONG ISLAND, U.S.A.

That ever-glamorous New Yorker C.Z. Guest lives in old-world splendour surrounded by the marvellous riding country which she and her late husband Winston Guest, the famous polo player, loved so much. Here is the fine double avenue of old trees leading to the house, which perfectly captures, to my mind, that air of immense elegance and dignity that surrounds the area.

Edwin Whitney-Smith's figure of a young girl, cast in 1911, kneels among Louisiana irises and green arums.
The pool is on the far side of the slave bell, away from the main lawn.

An avenue of Australian gum trees frames one of the main drives into Brenthurst, providing welcome
shade on a hot African afternoon.

154

BRENTHURST
SOUTH AFRICA

The great garden of Mr. and Mrs. Harry Oppenheimer captures perfectly the enormously civilised style of the South Africa that I first knew 40 years ago. The slave bell in the background forms the focal point from the house, with a Renoir statue in front it.

The main lawns, as seen from the main house, with the slave bell in the distance.

The sunk garden at Rustenberg, so evocative of the British colonial garden, forming small, intimate spaces of colour, scent and cooling shade within the wide spaces and hot, dramatic landscapes of the erstwhile Empire.

The semi-circular front steps at Rustenberg are made of *klompte* bricks imported from Batavia as ship ballast in the days of Dutch East India Company rule. Here *Erigeron karvinskianus* seeds itself freely in the cracks, a Gertrude Jekyll gardening conceit introduced to the Cape by Sir Herbert Baker.

RUSTENBERG

THE CAPE, SOUTH AFRICA

The marvellous garden at Rustenberg is the 50-year-old creation of Mrs. Pam Barlow. A long walk to the end of the double border is rewarded by a stone bench which cleverly returns the viewer's gaze, presenting this unexpected *coup d'oeil* of the vista punctuated by the cypress trees and the Cape mountains beyond.

NOORDHOEK
THE CAPE, SOUTH AFRICA

The terraced garden at Noordhoek, the Herbert Baker house of Mr. John and Lady Sarah Aspinall, has had its gravel paths defined by great sweeps of lavender *angustifolia* suggested by Graham Viney who helped restore both house and garden.

Mr. Aspinall has succeeded spectacularly in eradicating invasive aliens among the Cape heaths and ericas which flower profusely on the surrounding mountains.

Facing. The main terrace at Noordhoek showing the great terracotta pots of marguerites, the lavender and bold plantings of roses.

Situated on a terrace high above the flowering gums
and distant sea views, the new herb garden to the west
of Noordhoek is a series of squares and circles, in
keeping with the established gardens in the
Jekyll/Baker style. Standard pomegranates grow
through terracotta pots. Household laundry is spread to
dry on the camomile lawn.

The cascade, fed by mountain streams, enters a stone
lily pond whose Baroque shape has echoes of the old
Dutch gardens of the Cape.

Facing. The great curved herbaceous borders, formed
above the croquet lawn by Lady Chaplin in the 1920s,
have been replanted with a predominantly pink and
grey colour scheme to match the coral wash of the
house itself. Here clumps of cleome, delphiniums,
hollyhocks and dahlias ('Gerrihoek') are carefully
planned to peak on Christmas Day.

BANTRY STEPS
CAPE TOWN, SOUTH AFRICA

Designer Graham Viney removed the ugly windows that enclosed the veranda of his post-First World War villa. Following the principle of the ha-ha, a ledge three feet below obviates the need for railings. From within, the views are unimpeded and the exhilarating effect is of a drop straight into the sea. The result is cultured, exotic, hugely dramatic and utterly relaxing.

BROADLANDS
THE CAPE, SOUTH AFRICA

The Hon. Patricia O'Neill still lives on the stud farm established by her mother the Countess of Kenmare at Sir Lowry's Pass in the Cape. Banks of white agapanthus line the drive to the old colonial homestead, nestling easily in the shadow of the mountains beyond.

The garden at Broadlands was laid out with advice from Mrs. O'Neill's brother, the late Rory Cameron, whose great sense of style was one of the moving influences of my own early work.

In a typically exotic scene, a peacock displays among the heavy-scented daturas of the Cape summer.

NEW BEACH ROAD

SYDNEY, AUSTRALIA

Designer Michael Love has made a hugely chic and restrained statement in urban living in the garden of his house at Darling Point. The pool is a good colour, the surround of a good stone. I love the careful 'random' placing of the stone bust beside it. The bulbous urns with their tiny balls of box are on absolutely plain pedestals. The wall is plain rendered and a marvellous contrast to the romantic abundance of the jasmine that falls down it. Objects are placed on the table with care and decision. The effect is theatrical and dramatic.

BOLOBEK
VICTORIA, AUSTRALIA

The greatest gardener on the Australian continent is without a doubt my friend Lady Law-Smith. I visit Australia every year and it is always a huge pleasure to visit Joan in her famous garden at the base of Mount Macedon, in the country outside Melbourne, and compare notes on our current enthusiasms. She has published prolifically and her garden is so well-known that I have included only one picture, this marvellously simple shady walk lined with forget-me-nots, daffodils and plane trees.

CRUDEN FARM
VICTORIA, AUSTRALIA

Dame Elizabeth Murdoch lives on this beautiful estate with a fascinating garden laid out by Edna Walling in the 1930s. It has all the charm, elegance and atmosphere of great colonial houses everywhere, an aura of times that are now, sadly, gone forever.

In the walled garden at Cruden Farm deep herbaceous borders run simply down each side, their lines echoed by the magnificent trees beyond.

Facing. One of the most beautiful approaches to any house, the drive to Cruden Farm is lined with wonderfully atmospheric *Eucalyptus citriodora* trees.

MOUNT MACEDON
VICTORIA, AUSTRALIA

Kevin O'Neill has created, over the last 15 years, a dream-like fantasy garden, at moments restrained and almost formal, at others exuberant to the point of wildness, like a magic forest in a Victorian fairy tale.

Against the south wall of the house are standard azaleas in good terracotta pots on mossy brick paving. Shade is provided by the pergola of Banksiae roses which sprawl and clamber towards the house.

Facing. The steps from the main lawn down to the forest and stream at the end of the garden are framed by two recumbent figures on pedestals and an overarching 'Strawberry Tree' (*Arbutus undeo*) which acts as a gateway to the enchanted forest below.

Further into the forest at Mount Macedon tree ferns shade a carpet of forget-me-nots and a lone, lost urn.

Facing. Before reaching the stream at the bottom of the garden, Kevin O'Neill built this little pavilion which he uses occasionally for small dinner parties. Lost in the forest of tree ferns it has an enchanting quality.

A 19th century English cast iron fountain stands as a central feature to be seen from the house, in a hexagonal pool of waterlilies surrounded by *Lonicera nitida* and set on a low platform of Queensland sandstone paving. Behind is the line of pleached pears that borders the property.

BRIGHTON

MELBOURNE, AUSTRALIA

Before meeting Paul Bangay 10 years ago, the only gardeners I knew, whose feeling for design and planting I could totally relate to, were not only much older than me but also extremely well known: Alvilde Lees-Milne, John Fowler, the Duchess of Beaufort, Russell Page, Roderick Cameron, Nancy Lancaster and Vita Sackville-West. Paul is one of their calibre, a designer whose work has a discipline, simplicity and style that comes from an eye rather similar to my own. This garden, designed by Paul for Mr. and Mrs. Glen Morley, shows exactly that style.

The swimming pool, designed to be looked down on from the upper floor of the house, with the simplest of pavilions, ochre coloured, strictly classical and symmetrical. The pool, surrounded by Queensland sandstone, is hidden from the entrance, being two steps below the lawn, and set against eucalyptus trees.

GREEN OAKES AVENUE
SYDNEY, AUSTRALIA

Lady Finley, the neighbour of my first and best Australian friend, Lady Pagan, on Darling Point outside Sydney, has an idyllic garden that is very Italian in feeling. It is like a fragment of an early Renaissance painting brought to life, magically, in the southern hemisphere. The careful, rather elaborate placing of all the elements, each quite separate from the other, makes this a deeply contemplative garden; its style of green architecture is completely in my own taste.

The paired round arches, the smoothly rendered walls, the multitude of pots and vases on pedestals and the compartmenting with low hedges all add to the Renaissance feeling of this wonderful garden.

Facing. A rambling, brick-paved walk, lined by English box domes and *Clivea miniata* leads to a stone urn on a simple pedestal.

175

A Victorian iron urn holding tightly bunched local succulents at Green Oakes Avenue.

One of the blind arches of Lady Finley's house which are filled with *Ficus pumila* creeper, a Della Robbia medallion in the spandrel. I love the placing of the various small pots, one centred grandly in the arch, another centred on the column, the rest scattered randomly. Games of symmetry and asymmetry like these at Green Oakes Avenue are always an exercise and a delight for my eye.

Facing. Mrs. Herda's green 'sofa' of clipped box, with a hedge of *Choisya fernava* behind clipped tight to give a rounder shape, and huge camellias behind that. In front of the 'sofa' santolina is clipped low in stone paving. In each corner of the 'room' stands a *Laurus nobilis* standard.

PIBRAC AVENUE
WARRAWEE, AUSTRALIA

Prudence Herda has one of the most stylish and inventive gardens that I know. I have always enjoyed the idea of an architectural garden of 'green rooms', probably because of my work in interiors, but Mrs. Herda has made something truly extraordinary at her home near Sydney. The bench, with wooden seat but entirely filled below and behind with box, and with box arms, is a unique creation.

The swimming pool at Woollahra, between Espie Dods's corbelled brick walls, is extended cleverly by two huge plates of mirror-glass in the end wall. Star Jasmine, hiding the sides of the mirror, completes this illusion of doubled space.

To one side of the courtyard garden, overlooked by a balcony from the drawing room, the Laws created this little sandstone pool filled with waterlilies and fish. In the centre is a chunk of rock that they found at their country house, drilled to create the simplest of fountains, a single, narrow jet.

Facing. Looking out from the loggia of the house over the courtyard garden to the gate on to Queen Street. Garages each side of the gate are covered by masses of white wisteria and giant Burmese honeysuckle (*Lonicera hildebrandtiana*); the central space is defined by stepped box hedges, standard 'Iceberg' roses and a huge *Magnolia grandiflora*.

WOOLLAHRA
SYDNEY, AUSTRALIA

Caroline and John Laws have created several marvellous gardens in Australia, but it is this small town garden in Sydney that I admire most. The house was restored for them by our mutual friend, architect Espie Dods, and in the courtyard between it and busy Queen Street on which it sits, the Laws made this wonderful little oasis of calm, taking inspiration from the Italian Renaissance idea of the *giardino segreto* of a town palace.

GODDFREY HOUSE

HONG KONG

It always gives me intense pleasure to discover something new and sophisticated, especially when far from home. Mr. Goddfrey's garden on The Peak in Hong Kong is just such a find. Up above the noise and ugliness of this crowded city, which was once so lovely, as were so many of our old colonial centres, is this oasis of tranquillity and style.

On a hot evening the air up here is still cool enough to warrant the flaming brazier, a suitably exotic touch among the disparate elements gathered together so artlessly: the smart blue cushions on the bamboo furniture, the bonsai, so perfect here, so out of place inside, the massively overscaled pot.

DICTATION AND VARIETY
MY OWN WORK AS A GARDEN DESIGNER

My clients, like a doctor's patients, fall into several categories. I can often identify them by their initial approach. They are all wonderful and their sometimes totally different attitudes interest me. Some are dedicated plantsmen, some uninterested in the plant material, merely wanting a strong, stylish effect and, of course, there are many in between-ers.

I say they are wonderful because I am always flattered that they want me, and because they tend to treat me as a specialist they invariably agree to my diagnosis and remedy or operation.

With one of my American clients a particular piece of my advice has been categorically rejected over 18 months. It's all to do with a concrete balustrade between her lawn and a large lake. Whether it stays or goes on my advice would have little effect on the garden design but I do want it to go! However much people want to be told what to do, or 'dictated to', I always have to remember that it is their garden!

I think that clients know fairly accurately what kind of garden they will get if they come to me but I sincerely hope, and actually believe, that I create an entirely different ambience in two English gardens because the terrain, situation and soil are bound to be different, as well as existing features, like a mature tree or a river, which must of course exert their influence on the garden. So, indeed, must the house and outbuildings, let alone the clients' preferences. So the attitude and style may be somewhat similar, but the result will always be quite unique.

Naturally when I am designing in the Dominican Republic the result will be quite different to Michigan, and a small London garden in London S.W.1. entirely different to a largely public garden for my Livery Company in the City of London.

Variety has certainly been the spice of my designing life and it has brought a freshness and utter contrast to the job. The creative amongst us are very fortunate indeed – I could never work in the same office, year in, year out – because we are able to make magic, at least sometimes.

The different people for whom I have worked for 44 years have indeed been varied. Most, even from my mid-20s, have been really good to work with and a few have become great friends, but even in my 15 years working in this green and gentle garden world, two or three have been quite incompatible, which I find very sad.

Clients really want absolute decisiveness, in design principles and in selectiveness of flowers, trees and style. I truly value the trust that people put in my ideas: at least they can rely on one's experience, knowing what the end result will be; and they do appreciate a safe pair of hands.

I have had a hand in the design of the next four gardens: three are set in the English countryside, one right in the very heart of the City of London, surrounded by high-rise office buildings.

The centre of the Great Terrace at Harewood, recently replanted by Lord and Lady Harewood following Barry's original design, looking out over the vast composition of Capability Brown's park and lake beyond. The statue is 'Orpheus' by Astrid Zydower.

One of the seats which terminate the Great Terrace with my planting of limes and alchemilla behind.

Facing. The parterre on the Great Terrace, laid out by Sir Charles Barry in the mid-19th century, ends in generous semi-circular stone seats with Cupids frolicking on pedestals. I proposed planting behind these to give architectural emphasis and a sense of intimacy to the seats, using pleached limes with a froth of *Alchemilla mollis* at their feet.

HAREWOOD HOUSE

HARROGATE, ENGLAND

The Earl and Countess of Harewood are among the few owners of great houses who continue to embellish them. They have revitalised the house and also done wonderful things outside, among them replanting Sir Charles Barry's marvellous parterre on the Great Terrace. I helped with two parts of the garden, which are shown here, and also designed a rather elaborate 'teaching garden' to be built within the old kitchen garden which remains, so far, unachieved.

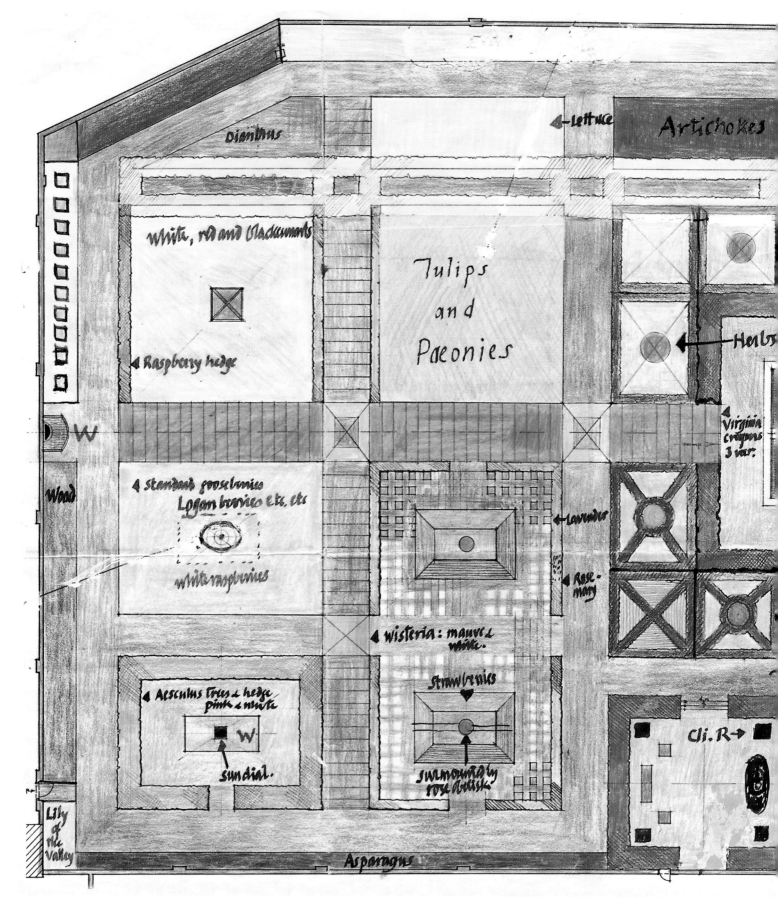

The 'teaching garden' that I conceived for the Harewood's largely disused kitchen garden. They were inspired by a visit to Villandry, always one of my own first points of reference, and wanted to do something with this large space. My design combined the ingredients of vegetable, fruit and flower gardens in a complex geometric

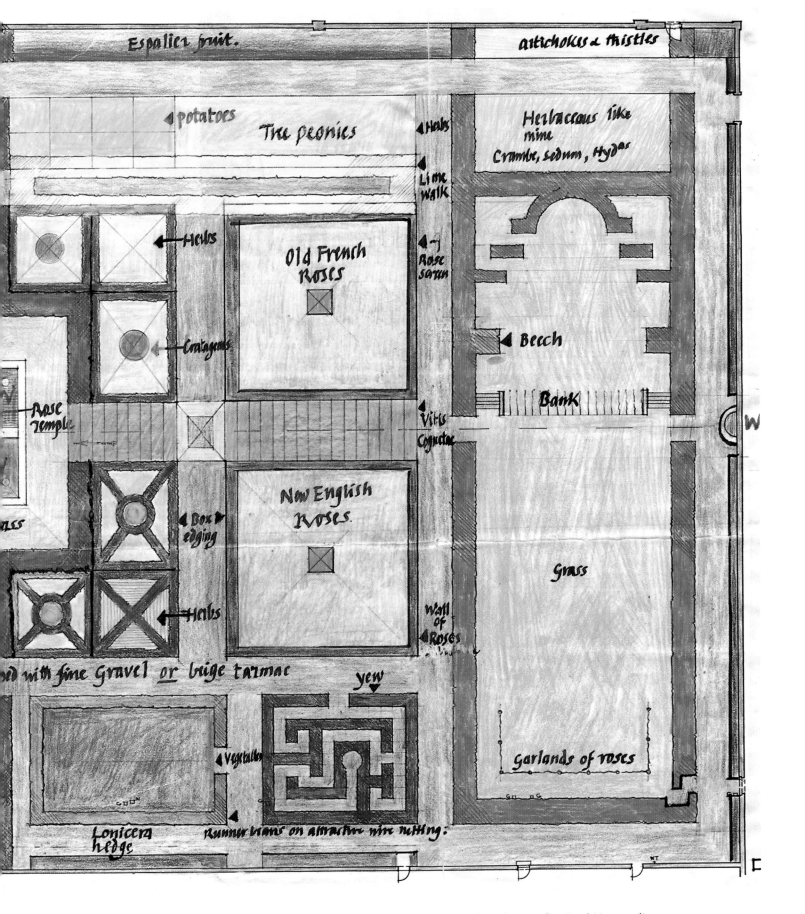

plan which included a large 'green theatre' (complete with wings, to the right, to reflect Lord Harewood's passion for opera), and unusual features like the pyramids of strawberries which would set the fruit at perfect picking height.

A letter I sent to Lord and Lady Harewood in March 1990

I post this between Rio and Faro so that you will know that I have not forgotten the project . . . I see it as a 'teaching garden' [see previous pages]. I'm so intrigued by what I have conceived that I might apply for the job of Head Gardener! I think it's subtle. I know it's too complicated but it <u>can</u> be simplified. There isn't a garden, anywhere, like it <u>could</u> be. It isn't Castle Howard or Villandry. It's Harewood!

It has contour, texture, water, scent, shape, pattern and <u>no</u> colour. It's formal but it has irregularities. It has flowers, but in edited colours. The plan is of a main vista, looking down, of hornbeams with a *pièce d'eau* in the centre and, at right angles, two walks – one tunnel of *Vitis coignetiae* and the other of pleached limes. It would be on three levels.

There are espaliered fruit trees, lavender beds edged with clipped rosemary, a yew maze, a strawberry garden, a red- white- and black-currant <u>room</u> hedged in by raspberries. There could be a Paeony room – tree & herbaceous. I like the idea of an exhibition potato garden – how many varieties? Then I feel old French roses and new English roses and I wondered (to cut the labour down a bit) about a green theatre with walls & wings, etc. of Beech. Shall we meet in London to discuss it all?

Another view of my planting of pleached limes and alchemilla around the stone seats on the Great Terrace.

Facing. The Dolphin Garden on the upper section of the West Terrace at Harewood, which I conceived as a small, private 'room' within the larger garden, where one could sit and look out at the breathtaking landscape beyond. Stilt hornbeams and hornbeam hedges surround the octagonal pool.

As a central feature, I contrived a simple and slightly rustic fountain of a rough stone-edged pool with a stone base and this tremendous heraldic rendering of the company's crest and shield in bronze.

Facing. The garden has a simple geometric form but is a riot of romantic planting of roses on metal frames in summer, contrasting excitingly with the surrounding modern buildings.

SALTERS' HALL
CITY OF LONDON, ENGLAND

Male members of my family have belonged to The Worshipful Company of Salters for many generations; I was Master of the Company in 1977, like my father before me. I decorated the new Hall, built to designs by Sir Basil Spence, and more recently laid out a garden behind it, enclosed partly by the original Roman brickwork of the city wall. This has given me huge pleasure, and is much enjoyed by office workers from neighbouring buildings who come to eat their sandwiches on the benches provided.

A long path of well-fed lawn runs the length of this little green oasis in the midst of contrasting modern buildings and the wonderfully textural Roman city wall. Between beds of box, lavender and hostas are many of my favourite roses including 'Albertine', 'May Queen' and 'Constance Spry'.

WEST WYCOMBE PARK
WEST WYCOMBE, ENGLAND

Few things in life make me really jealous. My friend Sir Francis Dashwood, who lives quite near us in the most maddeningly beautiful park and house, built by his eccentric ancestor of Hellfire Club fame, succeeds. Who could not envy such splendid surroundings? The house and park are so well-known that here I show only two features, a bridge that I built and a charming little secret garden, absolutely to my taste, hidden away beside the house.

The new bridge which I built for Sir Francis Dashwood with the lovely Lady Dashwood's intial 'M' framed in its joinery. Its design was based on one drawn by Lord Burlington for his own garden at Chiswick, seen by Sir Francis in an old view of that famous garden.

Facing. A quite different view of West Wycombe from the lake, temple and broad stretches of picturesque landscaping that are so well known. To the south of the house, hidden away, is this delightful small garden I created in the 1960s with the help of Ross Brittain, who laid it out and designed the Chinese Chippendale gate, and Russell Page who was responsible for the planting. It has a character of such intimacy and charm, so typical of the small, private English garden, so different to the very public landscape all around.

DEENE PARK
CORBY, ENGLAND

I was asked in 1990 by my friends Mr. Edmond and the Hon. Mrs. Brudenell, who are fortunate enough to live in this staggeringly beautiful house, to suggest a new garden that they could see from the house. Mr. Brudenell's late father had always refused to allow anything other than grand expanses of lawn, feeling that flowers were only really suitable for cottages.

Plans of the 1640s show a huge formal garden to one side of the house, now, sadly, vanished. In its place is Brownian picturesque landscaping, parkland dotted with artfully arranged clumps of good trees, a stretch of man-made water and dense woods, but really no garden to speak of.

Inspired in part by the old formal garden, we laid out a new parterre between the house and the lake below, stretching the full length of the great façade, to be enjoyed from every window on that side. To my mind it captures somehing of the spirit of the 17th century while having a graphic modernity that is very much of the 20th century.

On an aerial snapshot I sketched the basic form of the parterre and noted my clients' instructions, 'low upkeep' and their comment on the existing profusion of lawns, 'too much mowing'.

Facing. The new parterre seems to me to sit quite naturally between the house and the lake below. The 40-year-old borders beside the steps are very much in sympathy with my new planting of box, lavender and nepeta, surrounding metal frames for climbing plants.

192

Looking down from the house on the just-planted beds of the new parterre. I was very conscious of the contrast of my rigorous formality with the 'natural' landscaping of lake and parkland beyond, which I find historically interesting and rather stylish.

My plan for the new parterre at Deene Park. Graphic simplicity with centres based on the two existing sets of steps down from the house. I always look for the existing structure of the site to give a rhythm and sense to my new design.

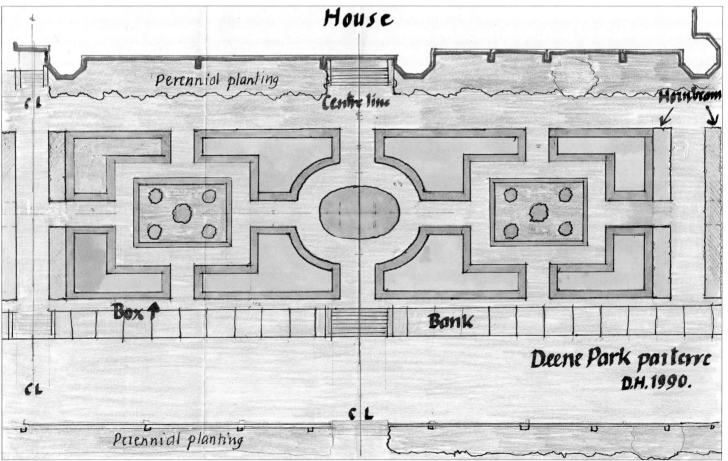

House

Perennial planting

Centre line

Hornbeam

Box

Bank

CL

Deene Park parterre
D.H. 1990.

Perennial planting

CL

FOREIGN CLIMES
GARDEN DESIGNING ABROAD

People are often amazed when I tell them that I am off to South Africa to design a garden in Johannesburg and then to the States to do another on the shores of Lake Michigan. They imagine that it must be very complicated because of the huge differences in climate to northern Europe, the totally different selection of available plants, and so on.

In fact, it is fairly straightforward. First I need to understand the local climate out of the several extremes possible within vast continents like Africa or the Americas.

At the outset, as I do with every new commission, I go into the house and look out from the windows of living room, dining room and main bedroom; only then do I go out into the garden, immediately visualising what should be seen from those three important rooms. This approach comes from England, where the weather dictates that most of one's enjoyment of a garden is from the house, but it holds good everywhere.

Next, I ask to be taken to the best local nursery garden. Within 30 minutes I get a pretty sure idea of what plants and trees I can use in that particular part of the world, of what the soil is, what the rainfall and the highest and lowest temperatures can be.

It is always essential to work with a reliable and accommodating garden contractor, for they can make or break my conceptions. I have been exceptionally lucky with those I have found. As in all structural undertakings the contractor is vital. Generally I find that most people in the garden world are gentle and sympathetic.

Working in different climates does necessitate varied approaches and attitudes to the garden, dictated by different plants and climates from one's own. My personal style, my love of strong, formal lines, my vision of architectural, almost wholly green, gardens of series of 'rooms', all this is no more difficult to create in any part of the world than in my Oxfordshire home.

VILA VERDE
ALGARVE, PORTUGAL

I think all designers inevitably have one great project which is their *chef d'oeuvre* and which they hope will remain as their monument. Certainly mine is the Palladian villa in Portugal for which I chose the site, designed the architecture, interiors, fabrics, furniture, and finally, the garden. It is my total creation and one that gives me a unique satisfaction and pleasure.

My clients, Amin and Nahid Ghani, immensely cultured and sympathetic people who became very great friends of ours in the course of the project, made the enterprise hugely enjoyable and challenging. Their generosity extends to my having a room of my own in the house, which leads me to spend enough time there to enjoy my creation and go on adding to it. It is, I think, a quite unique situation in the history of patronage.

When we started to plan the house, Madame Ghani and I travelled together to many of those parts of the world that I have always loved and found inspiration in. We saw many places, from my neighbours' gardens in England to the Moghul Garden in Delhi. We also explored the Algarve and other parts of Portugal, everywhere seeking – and finding – inspiration and excitement for our great project.

The house was completed in 1986. The first parts of the garden were formed then: the sunken rose garden and the swimming pool. Over the following twelve years we have added to it. The project has only been possible because of the vision and sympathy of my clients and friends, for which I will always be very grateful.

The house and garden style I created resonates with the simplicity and the strength of line I would describe as being representative of my signature. Both house and garden work one with another, and with the site, each part enhancing the other to make a complete design statement. Increasingly, my clients understand that no matter how small their outdoor space, it does not exist in isolation and that the interior and exterior are inextricably linked.

My sketch for a screen wall to part of the garden, with framed openings to the spectacular views of the distant Atlantic ocean, to be plastered with the same rough, textured *impasto* finish as the house itself, made of sand, cement, colour and sea shells from the local beaches.

Facing. The drive climbs up the property to the house, which sits atop a small hill with commanding views. In deliberate contrast to the formal classicism of the façade, inspired by Inigo Jones' 'Tuscan Barn' church at Covent Garden, I left the planting very loose, with white oleanders under plane trees.

A rather severe architectural water feature at the Vila Verde is designed to be seen from the Staircase Hall, its sound deliciously cooling on a hot Portuguese day.

Facing. The water feature has been softened over the years by the equally delicious fruit-bearing bananas that have grown up beside it.

Behind the house I have made trellis ceilings, across which wisteria is beginning to grow, to give shade and scent in the hot midday. Classical urns on simple pedestals hold cacti, while lavender in pots and climbing roses on the wall of the house add to the scented atmosphere.

Facing above. The sunken rose garden was one of the first parts of the garden to be laid out at Vila Verde, its dimensions copied from part of the Moghul Garden in Delhi. I ordered old English roses, among them 'Queen of Denmark', from my favourite supplier at home and was amazed at how well they did under the fierce sun.

Facing below. The second sunken garden, beyond the pool, with plumbago climbing the walls and rows of white petunia in pots.

My working sketches for the Vila Verde fountain.

Facing above. To give a focus to the dining terrace below the portico, I built a fountain, of angular geometric design, in cement with local sea shells. Around it are eight slender spikes of trellis with blue plumbago.

Facing below. The Vila Verde swimming pool, seen from the house, with the deep blue of the distant Atlantic ocean glimpsed below the umbrella pine and behind the statue, a British Museum cast of the Greek 'Spear Bearer'.

I have for many years noisily decried the horror of pink bougainvillea, swarming as it always does so predictably over every available surface in sunny southern climes from the Caribbean to Lake Como. At Vila Verde, we had already used some of the much prettier white variety.

Two years ago, I suddenly had a vision of Indian pink parasols from an elephant parade, and these gave me the inspiration for my bougainvillea umbrellas, the hitherto offending pink blossom spilling over metal frames standing in wooden boxes planted with lavender and herbs. At the end, a trellis pyramid with two shady seats (right).

A gardener's doodle recording some of the ideas I had while at work at Vila Verde.

204

RIVERSFIELD FARM
KWAZULU-NATAL, SOUTH AFRICA

Some five years ago I was asked by Neville and Helen Schaefer to design a garden for them at their country house outside Durban. In an area of incredible beauty, with a vast, rolling landscape, I was given a free hand. I designed a small brick pavilion with Gothic windows and a hipped roof, rather Chinese in profile, and a clean, rectangular swimming pool enclosed by 'walls' of green. Elsewhere are lines of good trees and scattered smaller structures dotting the landscape in the manner of the 18th century English garden.

Facing. Looking out from the pavilion, across the pool to the landscape beyond.

The pavilion, framed by square-cut viburnum hedges, with the utterly simple, tile-edged pool in front.

A thatched Doric-style pavilion I designed for the garden at Riversfield Farm.

Facing. A small trellis-roofed shady seat of my design. This dominates a secluded corner with a more intimate scale of space and planting. The success of a garden design can often depend on finding exactly the right balance between wide open spaces and smaller, more personal ones. The design of the building is simple in the extreme but the details I find hugely satisfying, from the size of the acorn finial to the curve of the brackets.

STELLENBERG
KENILWORTH, SOUTH AFRICA

Having always loved the romance and other-worldliness of the Cape Dutch homesteads of South Africa, it was a huge pleasure to me to be asked by Mr. and Mrs. Andrew Ovenstone, owners of this particularly beautiful house, to design a garden for them some years ago, for their twenty-fifth wedding anniversary. Even more so since Mrs. Ovenstone herself is a very keen and talented gardener who had already created a large and elaborate garden, a series of 'rooms' very much in my own style, including a hugely stylish White Garden next to the house.

The rich Baroque forms of the house's roofline, and that marvellously austere style of white stucco and small-paned windows, characterise the old Dutch colonial house.

Facing. From the dining room, an ingenious arrangement of sash and doors opens on to the White Garden that the Ovenstones created. Every kind of colourless flower: roses 'Iceberg', 'Blanc Double de Coubert', 'Fair Bianca'; zinnias and giant white cactus dahlias in summer; white tulips, stocks, irises, primulas and violas in spring; Cape hyacinths and foxgloves; all within an edging of white oxalis and peppermint-scented pelargonium.

210

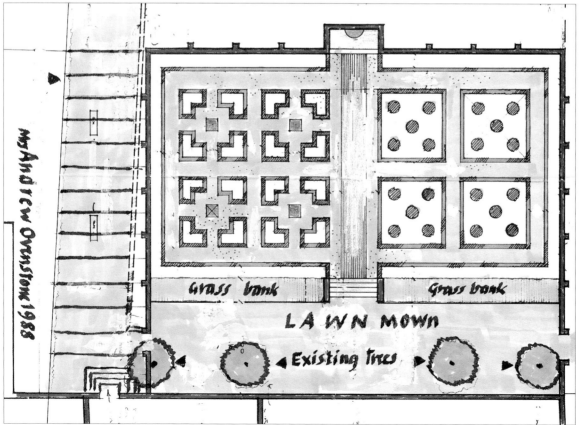

The Walled Garden I made at Stellenberg soon after it was planted in 1989, showing the determined, geometric structure of the design.

My original plan for the Stellenberg garden, in an old walled enclosure that had contained a little-used tennis court. The total simplicity of the scheme, divided into two by a brick path running to a fountain, with symmetrical but dissimilar square beds to each side, is typical of my design philosophy.

Facing. The garden in maturity: low hedges of clipped myrtle edge the geometric beds, while pyramid frames support climbing roses 'Iceberg' and 'Félicité et Perpétué'.

Grass bank   Grass bank

LAWN MOWN

← Existing trees →

Mr Andrew Ovenstone 1988

212

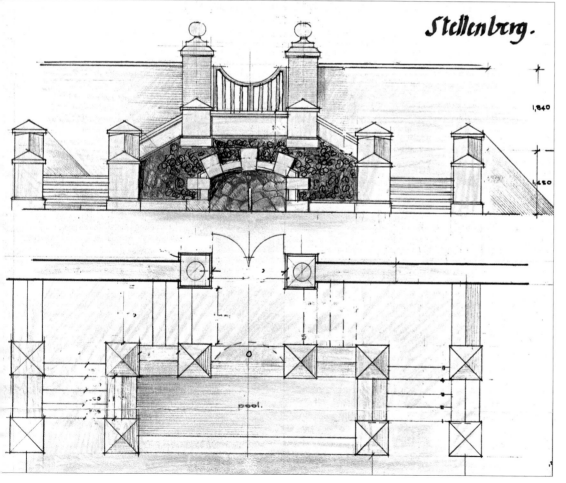

Stellenberg.

pool.

Above left. The swimming pool is set in the simplest and most restrained context, with a Chinese Chippendale pierced gate revealing the dramatic splendour of the mountains beyond the walls.

Above. A gate of my own design, leading to another of the garden 'rooms' at Stellenberg, which I have found equally suited to Oxfordshire, Florida and, here, the Cape.

Elevation and plan of my design for new steps and a water feature at Stellenberg, with a miniature, rocky grotto below the steps.

Facing. A brick path runs below arches festooned with 'New Dawn' roses along to the simplest of water features set in a recess on the far wall. The severe geometricality of my plan at Stellenberg is romanticised and softened by the gentle abundance of the planting.

HYDE PARK
JOHANNESBURG, SOUTH AFRICA

Six years ago, Mr. and Mrs. Donald Gordon asked me to design a large new garden for them at their new house in one of the greener areas of Johannesburg. The site contained nothing of any interest apart from a few old trees of good size outside the main area. I very quickly decided on a plan of crossing canals and geometric planting, a small pavilion in the distance reflected in the main canal, and a pair of splendid sphinxes on rusticated bases spewing water into basins below. The canals were inspired in part by the great Water Garden at Delhi, although their setting in green lawns gives a quite different effect.

From the steps that lead down from the house, an overview of the garden, the perspective centred on the little pavilion that terminates the long canal.

Facing. The graphic simplicity of the whole design is emphasised by the reflecting pool being the exact width of the pavilion it reflects.

In a corner of the garden, against the surrounding wall, is this little herb and rose garden centred on an old water cistern.

My plan for the garden at Hyde Park.

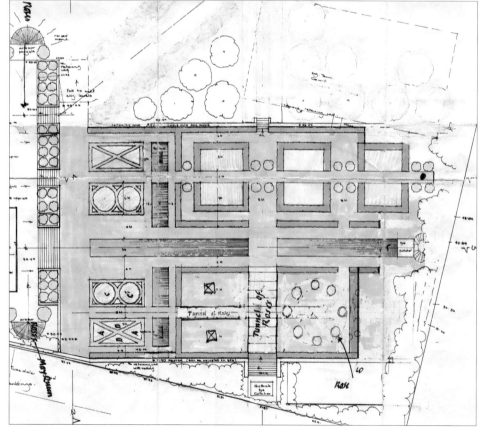

Facing. The garage at Hyde Park with tall standard bay trees in large painted Versailles planters of my design in serried ranks, giving the impression of a grand French orangery.

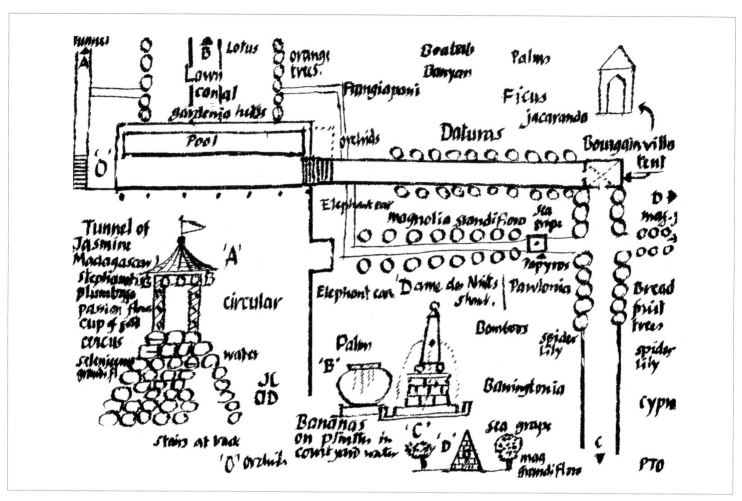

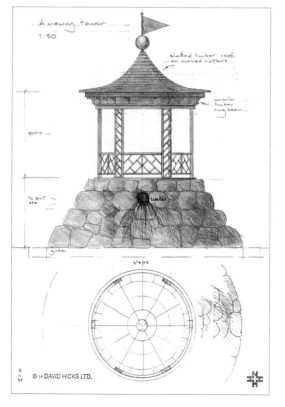

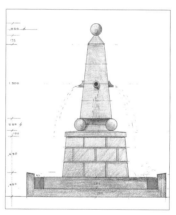

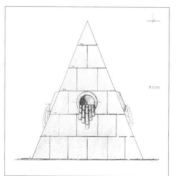

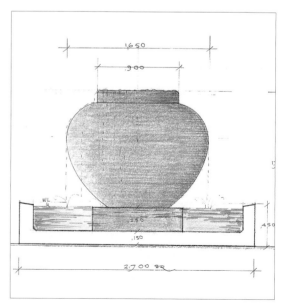

The initial rough drawing showing my ideas for Dana and John Scrymgeour's garden in the Dominican Republic, and the to-scale drawings of four of the features I designed to be situated in it: the pagoda, the obelisk, the pyramid and the great bowl.

EL INGENIO

CASA DE CAMPO, DOMINICAN REPUBLIC

David's voice on the phone: 'I've lost the travel directions; is the Dominican Republic near Ecuador?' Travel sorted, David arrived, clearly not in good health, and proceeded to design a most splendid garden with its own vistas as well as one of the distant sea.

True to his design notes and plan, in just one year (which included a hurricane with attendant damage) the garden has already begun to take shape as David intended. The grass is being cut, the tunnel is gradually being covered with vines, and the great bowl is in position (above).

Although there is still more to be done to complete David's vision of this garden, Dana and I are proud to have in the Dominican Republic this lasting tribute to an outstanding garden designer.   John Scrymgeour, July 1999

FURNISHING A GARDEN

An enormous problem which faces anybody planning a garden is how far they actually want to commit themselves to maintenance and upkeep in future. After all, those who do a garden, say in their thirties, have got a long life expectancy but somebody, like myself, who is making a garden at the age of fifty has got much less time and therefore one has got to plan the thing from the point of view of increasing old age and lack of help. It has to be planned in such a way that it can be cut back, in future years, into a manageable size. Romantic profusion, which has a great deal to contribute in garden design, can be allowed to go too far.

When planning a garden – or any part of a garden – try to envisage what it will look like if it is left partially untended. Some plants, as they become more abundant, can create a new and desirable effect. Trees as they grow larger become more dominant influences and they can be used to supersede other more time-consuming forms of planting. It is entirely possible to develop a garden from one which requires a great deal of time, worry and attention to one where, as the years advance, it is refined down to its few central elements, which can be maintained in their proper state with a much reduced expenditure of effort and money.

Often, from the ground, a garden seems completely regular, symmetric and formal, but from the air or on a drawing it is not. In planning my new garden I sometimes found myself becoming over-preoccupied with straight lines and having everything

A strong garden plan can transform the most pedestrian plot and careful planting can transform the most utilitarian building.

This stark situation needs a strong decisive attitude. Privacy and character can be acquired by planting hedges, climbing roses and by adding shutters and building a rustic arbour at the end of the drive. Beech is very quick growing if well fed.

at right angles; in dealing with old walls, I found that almost none of these were true. Allow the element of human error to creep in to the most formal of approaches. This gives a certain warmth to what could otherwise be too austere.

In the planning stage you must determine what is going to be used for what. If you have a young family, you will need an area where they can make a mess – where they can have playpens, slides, and their toys. Many people now think in terms of a swimming pool, even in very small gardens, so it is worth considering where you would put one, even if you are not going to have one straight away. Think also where things like the filtration plant and the heating unit would go; where you will keep the pool cleaning equipment. Are you going at some stage to want a tennis court? If so, it is a good idea to put up the netting now, and plant it with honeysuckle, so that at the time when you actually want to have the tennis court constructed, you already have it hidden – after all, they are very ugly and it then will no longer obtrude in your garden. If you are going to think ahead in this way, remember that contractors for pools and tennis courts arrive with large equipment – so do not build a wall or plant the area without provision for their access.

Croquet is popular with all ages, so part of your lawn may need to be sufficiently flat and large for this. Even in an existing garden you may find that the soil is not good all the way through, and it may be more economical in the long term to import some new topsoil rather than attempt to re-invigorate the poor existing soil.

The placing of garden seats and ornaments is very crucial and before I build a brick base for a container or an urn, I lay the bricks out dry and place the object on the base in order to see if three or four weeks later I am really satisfied that I have got the height right, and the dimensions of the base correct.

Hatred, Passion and Tolerance

I think it was being sent away to boarding school that started my critical reactions, pushing me to hate school dormitory sparseness, discipline, fir and silver birch trees as well as the dreaded rhododendron. I have a pair of tubs with 'Pink Pearl' rhododendrons in them, in an unimportant place, in order to remind me of how much I loathed going back to my prep school, Barfield. At a tender age a hatred was formed that has never been tempered.

I am afraid that, as I have grown older, my original hates have multiplied: turquoise swimming pools, rotating summer houses, sitting room-type conservatories, cement rabbits, irregularly shaped plastic ponds, paths and pools shaped like intestines, plant labels everywhere, hoses left out, crazy paving, wood stained a revolting orange, mini lanterns in wrought iron, orange or green floodlighting, asphalt paths, inexpensive wrought iron gates, and 'decorative' wells. White plastic garden chairs, grey gravel, bird baths, concrete balustrading, hanging baskets, and small fountains are all abominable.

In the plant world I have a loathing for flowerbeds, rockeries, aster, aubretia, almost all marigolds, tapestry hedges, arboretums, mixed avenues, orange lilies, forsythia, valerian, scarlet geraniums and salvias, aubergine-coloured shrubs, fuschia, lupins, Michaelmas daisy, red hot poker, lavatera, impatiens, snapdragons, begonia, Leylandii hedges, pampas grass, dahlias, gladioli, and the year-round commercial chrysanthemums.

I could happily do away with any variegated or bicoloured plants, shrubs and trees; it's their indecisiveness that I detest – they have been encouraged not to make up their minds. Really good herbaceous planting can be superb, as at Buckingham Palace or New College, Oxford, but on any less high plane, herbaceous borders are a nightmare and extremely labour intensive.

All this, however, is balanced by my ever-growing list of passionate likes.

I love *Rosa viridiflora*, 'American Pillar' rose, 'Mrs. Cholmondeley', 'Madame Boiselot', 'Madame Isaac Pereire', 'Constance Spry', and 'Lord Louis' (after my late father-in-law), indeed all roses except miniature ones and the County series. I long all year for the joy of June when my Secret Garden explodes into a heady scented paradise of roses, which sadly lasts only too short a time.

I love architectural gardens, clipped trees, long grass, wild flowers, yellow gravel, ground cover between roses, hollyhocks, pink and aubergine herbaceous poppies, tree and herbaceous peonies and sweet peas that really smell, which I like on wigwams of cane.

In the early part of the year I love snowdrops, aconites, bluebells (in woods only), *Hippeastrum amaryllis*, except for 'Picotee' and one or two others, fritillaries and crocus. I like all the narcissi family and hyacinths, which always remind me of Louis XV arriving for lunch at the Grand Trianon with the parterres all yellow with jonquils; when he emerged after lunch they were all pink with hyacinths!

Tulips are a lovely herald of the glories of colour to come and I delight each winter in ordering them. I especially like the smell, not a scent but a smell, of tulips; my favourite is Rembrandt.

I adore rhubarb (more delectable when growing than it can ever be for lunch on

Sunday), cabbages, onions, lettuces and all vegetables growing, especially artichokes, daisies on a lawn, hostas galore, honeysuckle, clematis, all forms of Russian vine, *Vitis coignetiae*, gunnera, crambe, paulownia, catalpas, *Heracleum giganteum*, espaliered fruit trees, yew (but not golden), hornbeam, beech, privet (not variegated or golden), lonicera, laurel, smooth-edged holly, copper beech (but never in the landscape or in a park), sunflowers, *Salvia turkesticana*, delphiniums in pots, allium, feverfew, rodgersia, inulas, bergenias, choisya, lavender, rosemary, autumn crocus and cyclamen.

I love ginger plants but they need heat. My darling Winnie (Countess of Portarlington), who never had a cut flower in any of her houses, had six of them, massed in a huge Korean dish. Zinnias, which I thought the world of as a child, I still like, but only the bright ones, and cut not growing. Plumbago is a great favourite and there it is in my greenhouse with daturas, jasmine and two geraniums growing up the wall.

Humea elegans is also lovely but it's not an easily available seed. I also love campanulas, ceanothus, phlox and orchids. Lilac and philadelphus, hellebores, gypsophila, camellias, hydrangeas, dianthus and *Phytolacca americana* all have important places in my garden.

I was determined that my list of hates should be shorter than my list of favourites because enthusiasm is far more important in gardening than negativeness, than complaining about one's soil and poor results. I have often had to remind myself that you cannot grow everything. Be adventurous, try many things and then spurn or discard; rule out certain plants if they don't work well with you. Stop being cross about your failures and concentrate on what grows well with you.

As a designer I like to control the scale, the variety, the texture and colour, the placing of different forms and shapes into a designed entity. The following pages illustrate some of the ways imaginative and coherent design can be introduced into different areas of the garden.

For this extremely small London back garden, I would make a definite statement, with a line of pleached and clipped hornbeam trees. The planting behind them would be with rhubarb and rheum, and the underplanting of the front with hostas. I would use a number of plants in flower pots and would break up the rather ordinary, concrete slab paving by making a panel of cobblestones.

Gateways define the entrance.

An interesting combination of brick and foliage at Frewen College in Sussex.

This gate and railings join the stable block to the main house at Tytherope Park.

Fine beech hedge surmounting an old brick wall.

Boundaries

The earliest gardens were contained for very practical reasons – privacy, exclusion of vermin, and to limit the area of cultivated ground. Walls were built as a protection for plants as well as for keeping out intruders. Very early on hedges of yew and holly were used to provide a sense of containment. Every detail of the garden plan and its perimeter must be decisive. The design you use for your entrance gate and the colour of the drive, the colour and texture of brick and mortar you use for a wall, the colour of the cement, which must be related to the type of brick, and the effect you intend, the sort of fence or hedge – all these elements are vitally important. In a sense, the boundaries and divisions are like the binding of a book – the handsome externals which announce a well-presented interior.

The most exciting element of a fence or hedge, or a wall, is its sense of continuity and of containing what you own or cultivate; and then the way it is pierced – by a simple opening with an arched head, or perhaps no top to it at all. With the gate or doorway, having it closed or left open leads the eye through to the space beyond. Successful gardens have variety of containment – long views, contrasting with small contained areas.

I am always looking for inspiration from other people's solutions when travelling around the countryside. If you are about to build a fence, or a wall, make a doorway, or plant a hedge, look and see what other people have done. For example, I was interested to see that the beech in the hedges at Drummond Castle are planted in a straight line only 5-6 inches apart, and are 16 feet high.

Good looking Edwardian gate and fencing in Nottinghamshire.

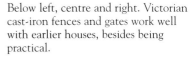

Left and far left. Fences made of simple painted palings give a delightful linear quality to the boundaries of small houses.

Below left, centre and right. Victorian cast-iron fences and gates work well with earlier houses, besides being practical.

Decorative pierced hedge at Gamberaia in Italy.

The Manor House, Bledlow.

An excellent example of a boundary hedge separating the cultivated garden from the countryside at Penshurst.

Topiary giving an interesting silhouette at Knighsthayes in Devon.

The walled garden at Crichel.

Dramatic battlemented wall at Penshurst in Kent.

A delightful pierced gate leading into a walled garden. White posts and chains are practical and decorative.

Boundaries should have apertures, to give access to and to look out of and beyond to other parts of the garden. This can be through a *clairvoyée* – a wide opening with metal railings, a doorway – of which there are infinite variations, or a simple gate, hedge or staggered arrangement of hedges. An element of drama is always introduced by an aperture.

A variety of gates and gateways, clockwise from above: Easton Grey, Canons Ashby, Le Petit Fontanille, Lord Tweedsmuir's garden, in the Vaucluse, Hidcote.

I formed this Gothic doorway in a barn to give access and a prospect on to a distant terrace in my own garden.

I pierced a wall in my garden to give access to a small garden beyond, and designed this simple spider's-web Chinese Chippendale softwood painted door.

Above. A dramatic doorway in Nancy Lancaster's garden at Haseley.

Far left. A cast iron trellis-panelled doorway in Lady Caroline Gilmour's enchanting riverside garden leads into Syon Park.

Left. A trellis gate hung from posts surmounted by wooden urns has great style.

Underfoot

The most obvious elements of gardens are the verticals – trees, tall plants, walls and hedges rising from the ground. But of equal importance are the horizontal areas, the expanse seen when sitting or standing in the garden or from the house. Too much mown grass or too many gravel paths can become monotonous. An excess of brick or flagstones can be arid and dead. As with the vertical elements of a garden, you must strive for variety in material and texture underfoot. What you use is going to be significant throughout the year, whatever the season.

Thyme planted between paving smells delicious underfoot. Aim for contrast, but not too much of it in designing your garden. And always consider what is on the ground.

Top. Radiating brick spokes with inset pebbles at Rofford Manor, near Oxford.

Centre. The Marchioness of Salisbury created this path combining cobbles and irregular stone centrepieces at Cranborne Manor.

Left. At Hatfield House cobbled treads and stone risers give a bold textural effect.

Far left. At Chatsworth, slabs of stone provide a practical surface in winter, between splendid beech hedges, incorporating caryatids from Chiswick House.

Left. A sense of perspective: a wide pathway flanked by trees at Bledlow Manor.

Far left. At Sissinghurst, looking from a slightly raised grass terrace edged in brick down on to a stone flag path also edged in brick, which is in turn edged in box.

Left. A brick and stone flagged path edged severely in clipped box.

Far left. Looking down from the top of the mount at Kew Palace; edged in box, the path is made of square cut stones.

Left. Guildford Bell, in his Melbourne garden, used brick underfoot in a generous, stylish way.

233

Change of level is also important, for it can break up a tedious flat expanse, and even under deep snow this is still effective. Steps are an ideal soluton in a garden on sloping ground. I like gravel paths and, with modern weed-killers, their upkeep is minimal. I know a number of people who reject the idea of a formal high-maintenance garden and achieve dramatic effect by having long grass, beautiful until mid-July, coming almost up to the house, cutting mown paths around the perimeter, and, through the long grass, leading to a glade or opening. When it is cut there is only an awkward two-week interval while it becomes green again, and it can then be rewarding for the whole of the rest of the year.

Stone paths and terraces are ideal. It is possible to buy second-hand paving stones, often from town councils, but at considerable cost. However, there are many concrete paving stones available which are quite acceptable. New textures and colours are being produced each year. I was lucky enough to find, under a thin layer of concrete in my backyard, several thousand cobblestones, which I have re-used to advantage as a border around my front door porch, on a geometric stone and cobblestone terrace and as the surround to the swimming pool. Second-hand cobbles can be bought, but it requires some skill to bed and lay them properly.

Before making decisions about your new garden underfoot, go and see some of the great small gardens that are open to the public, and the larger ones as well. Hidcote and Sissinghurst immediately spring to mind: see the various solutions that the great gardeners who created these found for the problems they faced – and which, in one form or another, you may face.

A combination of grass and gravel at Dumbarton Oaks, Washington DC.

York flags with a casual cottage-garden border spilling over.

Stone steps and pathway at Knightshayes.

Above. Random but large sections of stone form this romantic stairway in Provence.

Above right. John Mackenzie's garden at Cap Ferrat has herring-bone brick edged with pebbles. It makes an interesting textural effect.

Left. Le Petit Fontanille, St. Etienne du Grès, France.

Green Architecture

Stilts, Tunnels and Arbours

Villandry, Sissinghurst, Hidcote, The Hunting Lodge at Odiham – four great gardens where the green architecture of closely clipped walls and shapes has influenced and inspired me throughout my gardening life.

Although fairly labour intensive, the finished results, whether an ambitious, moderate or small scheme, are completely satisfying.

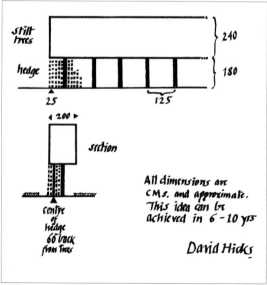

Top and above. In the Stilt Garden at Hidcote, Lawrence Johnston created one of the great masterpieces of garden design in England since 1900.

At The Grove I sketched a row of stilt trees on a photograph of the barn which I wanted to conceal. The photograph on the right shows the successful outcome.

Two diagrammatic sketches I have made showing exactly how to plan your stilt arrangement: width between each tree, height and depth you aim for, and so on. It is absolutely essential to prepare in this way, before you even think about doing the planting.

John Fowler planted these two lines of hornbeam in 1947 in his garden at The Hunting Lodge, Odiham. I first saw this garden in the early 1950s and it had an overwhelming influence on my garden thinking.

Left. A drawing I made of my first idea for the view from the drawing room window at The Grove. At the time I was not certain whether it should be chestnut or lime, settling in the end for hornbeam.

Far left. A simple architectural rustic pergola, on which old roses are trained. Stylish and attractive the year round, it would give structure to any garden.

Above and right. Arbours, walks and tunnels which form a covered walk provide a shady area which can be welcome on a hot day. Light and shade are closely related to texture.

Above. This shady arbour terminates in a delicate garden seat.

Right. An earthenware pot of good proportion provides a terminal point for this tunnel, which shows the effective contrast of light and shade.

Topiary and Parterres

One of the greatest examples of a 'shape' garden is Beckley Park. Apart from two climbing roses clinging to ancient apple trees, there is no colour in this garden other than every kind of green, which has 'Castle pudding' yews 30 feet high, yards and yards of box hedges, hornbeam garden temples, grass, mossy brick paths, and a small cutting garden hidden away behind yet more box hedging. It was all planted in 1924. This style of green architecture has an overwhelming interest for me, from the smallest clipped topiary shape – perhaps in a modest-sized container – to the most famous topiary garden in England at Levens Hall in Cumbria. The variety of shapes, both geometric and abstract, is almost limitless. These variations fascinate me, whether they are single animal shapes or vast sculptural blocks, extensions of the house, or boundaries or divisions between one part of the garden and another. Shapes can be formed into green buildings in their own right, and provide partial shelter in the midst of a summer storm. To achieve a proper shape for your green architecture often requires a concealed wooden or metal framework, as a certain amount of tying-in and support is needed. You must be decisive when you are working on such a project, and do remember the scale that you eventually want to arrive at. Feeding, weeding, watering and cutting are vital to good shaping.

Creeper covered wigwam for children.

Lord De L'Isle's green tent for Penshurst – ivy or virginia creeper clad.

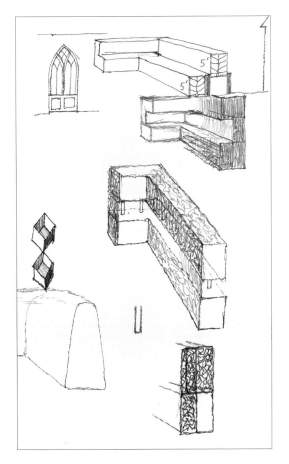

etcetera

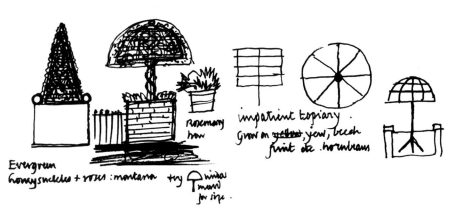

Evergreen honeysuckles + roses : montana

Rosemary bush

impatient topiary. Grow on yew, beech print etc. hornbeam

A small evergreen parterre planted by Roderick Cameron at Saint-Jean, Cap Ferrat, is full of enchantment.

Above and below. Mr. Basil Feilding's father planted these triumphs of topiary in Oxfordshire in 1924.

The large stone plant containers on the private terrace at Chatsworth are no longer filled with bedding-out plants but planted with box and yew.

The great yew rondel at Sissinghurst, planted in 1932, is a wonderfully contemplative area in which to rest the eye between the delights of the other parts of the garden beyond.

*Develope a sense of space
and compartments or rooms*

Right. The Duchesse de Mouchy in her garden in France has this enchanting box sentry box.

Below left. These phallic shapes rising out of square bases make an important contribution to the garden design at Hidcote.

Below right. In Mrs. van Rousmalen's garden, at Rekem in Belgium, there is a delightful topiary pavilion enclosing a seat. This green structure is *Cornus mas*.

Above. The magnificent parterre at Helmingham Hall, Suffolk.

Right. Dom Luiz Bramao's neat, ordered box garden at Vila Bramao in the Algarve.

Facing above. Baroque 'Parterre de Broderie' in the Queen's Garden, Het Loo Palace.

Facing below. The parterre at Fort Belvedere, designed by Arabella Lennox-Boyd, is a geometric arrangement of bedding surrounded by box hedging, with the central feature of a lead water cistern set in the midst of low planting and brickwork.

243

Textures

Some of the best gardens rely principally on texture for their effect – on the contrast of a hard line of flagstone with the softer but still sculptural lines of the clipped hedges, or the delightful interplay of large leafed plants with the smaller scale of box behind. Texture should be designed into a garden. It can remain constant throughout the year, or it may alter with the seasons. The textures of bare branches against a winter sky may be as striking and effective as full foliage in spring and summer.

Gunnera luxuriant by the lake at Syon Park.

Top left. Variety of texture in planting provides tremendous light and shade. Euphorbia, seen here above a plant of smaller habit, has excellent delineation.

Centre left. An explosion of foxgloves naturalised under trees in Oxfordshire.

Left. This summer tapestry comprises hosta, iris, thistle, and crambe against a yew hedge.

Textural contrast achieved by combining coniferous and herbaceous planting on the Kew rockery.

Far left. A minute garden pond, beautifully planted, stocked with fish, and looking inviting in the early summer sunlight. The contrast in textures of water, light and plants is most effective.

Left. In Christopher Lloyd's magical garden at Great Dixter, Sussex, mown grass and long grass are used in a masterly way. In the long grass he has encouraged many charming wild flowers.

Far left. At Cock Crow Farm John Stefanidis makes fine use of texture with gravel paths, low box and a taller planting of lavender.

Left. A large walled garden in Dorset is divided into huge beds containing fruit trees, vegetables and flowers, bordered with box, and grass paths edged with brick.

Far left. Silver-leafed edging looks delightful in this yew enclosed garden, planted with grey-silver and almond-green colours, including two standard eucalyptus.

Left. In Rory Cameron's garden near Menerbes his clever use of texture is seen here in the contrast of washed gravel, planting and stone walls.

At Kew cobblestones, box and grey planting provide superb and refined examples of textural contrast.

Yew and beech hedging in an exciting juxtaposition of textures at Hidcote.

At La Chèvre d'Or, Biot, a pebble path punctuates a variety of Mediterranean textures.

Left. Varying textures and heights give interest to this border at Tintinhull.

Below left. Bold clump of euphorbia at Kelmscott.

Below centre. Clipped olive trees with a tailored hedge beneath supported by a severe gravel path, make a perfect foil for the Mediterranean cypresses behind.

Below. Campanula and honeysuckle combining well on a June day in the west of England.

Water Features

Of all the elements in gardening water is probably the most significant. From the hot dusty plains of Rajahstan where the Moghuls made the most ingenious use of water ever conceived by mankind to the smallest suburban back garden where a simple jet in a pond can produce a romantic atmosphere, water delights us in any garden. People lucky enough to have a natural pond, lake or stream are, of course, in a totally different league. I myself live on rather dry high ground although I have regenerated an old horse pond, an absolutely vital element of pre-tractor farming. Here I have a limited number of water-loving plants – *Gunnera manicata*, for example – but used in a very natural way: it is not a botanical collection of water-loving plants. I have also used an old stone tank with a fine spout of water falling into it which is worked by a small electric pump recycling the water.

If you are able to create even the smallest pond, you can indulge in all the delights of the aqua plant world and of those foliage plants such as gunnera and other moisture-loving foliage plants.

I am not very keen on bog or water gardens in areas where they do not occur naturally. They can look very artificial.

A large formal pond on a terrace below the house at Bodnant in Wales.

A classical water feature at Compton Acres in Hampshire.

Reflections in a small yew-surrounded pool at Hidcote.

Top. The sunken pool at Great Dixter, Sussex.

Above. The elaborate series of canals on different levels which descend from Buscot House into the lake at this splendid National Trust property.

Right. An unusual water feature at Pepsico, White Plains, New York.

A long brick edged water-course at Chemin du Moulin, France.

Chemin du Moulin, Opio, France.

Below left. At the Château de Brantes water and trees have been used to give a delightful perspective in the garden of this beautiful house.

Below centre. At home in the country, I constructed this rusticated arch with a lion's head spilling water into a simple stone drinking trough. Knapped flint combines attractively with hostas in pots.

Below right. The Baronne Geoffroi de Waldener completed part of her garden in Provence with this marine mask from which trickles a gentle flow of water into a mediaeval rectangular container from which the water spills, in turn, into a large tank below.

In 1955, I restored the 18th century canal at The Temple in Suffolk which had silted up during the war.

Below. A canal at Villandry, well clad in water lilies.

Above right. A rather severe architectural feature I designed for the Vila Verde.

Below left. At Chatsworth, water bubbles up in a rhythmic flow from the centre of a large basin.

Below centre. The great canal at Chatsworth in Derbyshire, with the Emperor Fountain, designed by Paxton for the visit of the Tsar of Russia, is perhaps the greatest example of a man-made piece of water in Great Britain. The present Duke planted the splendid pleached limes in 1952.

Below right. The Bath of Diana at Penshurst Place in Kent. A splendid rectangular piece of water with a background of yew, and the ancient house and church beyond it.

Bridge with decorative balustrade.

Elegant curved arch at Helmingham Hall, Suffolk.

Massive classical stone bridge at Chiswick House.

Bridge with lake and temple beyond at Buscot Park, Oxfordshire.

Part of the naturalistic water features at Stourhead.

Elaborate drawbridge spanning a wide moat at Helmingham.

Swimming Pools

Swimming pools are a much neglected element from the point of view of really contributing to the garden design. Most people are inclined to think that swimming pools must be aquamarine blue and must be free-form in shape and only seen when the sky is blue, so they tend to be hidden behind ill-conceived rows of hideous macrocarpa hedging. At The Grove I have painted the swimming pool black so that it resembles a formal stretch of water. Aggressive but practical chrome steps are demountable and only put out for bathing weather. Confronted by the usual lack of imagination or sense of design by the pool contractor, I have clothed the white plastic covers to the filtration units with loose cobblestones, which look all part of the 12-inch band of cobbles set in a weak mixture of concrete which edges the reconstituted stone paving pool surround.

In an irregularly shaped, small garden in France, the widest part being by the house, I constructed a swimming pool which followed the shape of the garden, with the furthest end being narrower than the nearest end, and through false perspective, it made the swimming pool seem twice as long as it really was.

Site your pool carefully, out of the cold north-east winds, surround it with beech hedges, a wall, or clipped trees, though not close to the pool. Leave plenty of space for sunbathing, and hide the heating unit carefully behind a pool pavilion or in a nearby building.

Natural cement with the volume of the water produces a subtle colour, and dark blue or green can be sympathetic in northern climates, whilst white is effective in the Mediterranean and tropical regions.

The swimming pool at Anne Veits's house in the South of France.

Glass house to enclose a swimming pool

The swimming pool at Noordhoek, The Cape, South Africa.

Below left and right. The pool at The Cottage, Badminton, which cannot be seen from the house, even from the bedrooms, because of its clever placing and well-designed yew hedge. The pool has a natural cement finish and the volume of water produces a delightful grey-green colour. One side of the pool area is planted with white flowers and the result is one of the best swimming pool treatments in England.

At La Bastide du Roi, near Antibes, an amazing swimming pool: square with obelisks at each corner and a white marble figure reclining on a chaise-longue under a semi-circular arch. It is sited immediately below the centre of the house.

This formal basin of water constructed a few years ago at Kew Palace gives a splendid idea for a swimming pool; the central feature has water descending from it into the pool.

Above. This swimming pool at Woolahra, Sydney, is cleverly extended by two huge plates of mirror-glass at the end wall.

Below. The swimming pool at Fort Belvedere.

Structures and Pavilions

There are endless variations in old gardens to draw from. There are classical, Chinese, Gothic, rustic, Neo-classic and Baroque themes in the form of bridges, temples, orangeries, vineries, peach houses, dairies, rotundas, pagodas, 'umbrellos', covered seats, grottoes, arcades, game larders, tea houses, gazebos, in the great and small gardens the world over – all with a motif, style or conception to inspire us for garden buildings of today.

The siting of utilitarian things (tool shed, greenhouse and compost heap) must be as carefully considered as that of ornamental garden buildings and the planting of trees and shrubs. A garden building can be the important focal point just as a church spire can be an eyecatcher in a landscape. When I started work on the garden at The Grove, the tool shed and greenhouse were the first to be considered.

Of the mass-produced greenhouses, aluminium is the most practical, but I myself prefer painted or natural wood ones because they are more congenial to the other elements of the garden.

Masterpieces of greenhouse design were constructed in the last century, and many still survive. Some of the details – devices on the corners and ribs, fretwork and filigree on the roof-line – can be adapted to give today's greenhouse more character. I never erect a wooden cover for Calor gas cylinders without considering carefully the design and proportion, and a useful garden shed can have character and style simply by adding a pretty porch or a circular window. The colour of wood or paint should be carefully thought out. Choose one colour for all your garden paintwork. I chose very very dark green. Off-white, beige and dark blue are good alternatives.

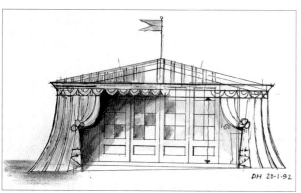

Above and left. Two of my drawings for garden pavilions.

Right. Pavilion at Riversfield Farm, Kwazulu-Natal.

This delightful Regency pavilion overlooks Lord Sackville's swimming pool at Knole.

Pavilion with bench seat.

Rustic pavilion, Lusthus, Sweden.

The garden of the King of Sweden at Ulriksdahl. This early 19th century openwork trellis pavilion of Gothic-Moorish design could be the starting point for a simplified version.

White Wood, Captain's Neck, Southampton, U.S.A.

257

Garden Furniture

Garden furniture is essential and particularly useful from a visual point of view. But it must be used with discretion. Too many chairs, benches or stools can look wrong. Permanent furniture like stone benches or seats must be clearly and thoughtfully positioned; there are delightful movable garden seats with wheels. Dining chairs and tables for summer garden living will need to be stored during the winter.

A delightful wheelbarrow seat at a house in Yorkshire.

Delicate Regency-Gothic garden chairs in wrought iron in the National Trust's most jewel-like garden, The Hunting Lodge at Odiham.

A typical Regency iron seat of great elegance.

A simple wooden garden seat.

At Cranborne Manor atmospheric Edwardian folding garden chairs.

John Stefanidis designed this stylish garden chair for his Dorset house.

Ornate bench on the great terrace at Harewood House.

A handsome Chinese Chippendale garden seat.

A charming variation on the wooden garden seat with slight Gothick influence.

A stylish white-painted piece of garden furniture.

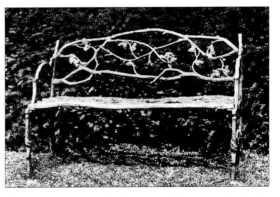

A wheelbarrow seat at Haseley.

Mrs. Lees-Milne set this iron seat on a small stone terrace and flanked it with symmetrical planting.

A romantic cast-iron Victorian garden seat at Beckley Park painted dark green in the all-green garden.

A curved seat in a shady corner at First Neck Lane, Long Island.

A pair of urns flank a charming garden seat of c.1910.

Wooden bench at Filoli, San Francisco, U.S.A.

A solid wooden seat at Sissinghurst, the base of which is clad with creeper.

A charming variation on Chinese Chippendale originally at Ditchley Park.

In the walled garden at Castle Howard, delightfully simple wooden benches in green alcoves.

Throne-like seat in a small wooden pavilion.

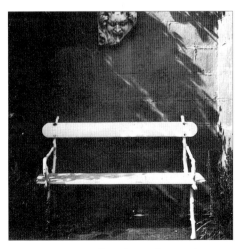

At Floors Castle, the Duke of Roxburghe has this delightful example of Edwardian furniture in natural wood.

A Victorian metal and wooden garden seat placed in a straight alcove in a new wall.

A delightful segmented seat surrounding the base of an old tree.

Garden Ornaments

Garden ornaments provide emphasis and accent in a garden, drawing the eye in a particular direction. Most ornaments, because they are solid and static objects such as urns, seats, columns or statues, provide a contrast with the living things around them. Ornaments can range from the simplest object – I recently spied a small concrete rabbit in the garden at Chatsworth – to the finest and most elaborate classical or 18th century statue on a contemporary base. They can be made of any substance, and although I have suggested that they are usually man-made, a natural object – a specimen tree (which is perhaps why they are known as ornamental trees) or a piece of topiary – can equally be a garden ornament. Seats and chairs have an ornamental quality as well as a purely functional one, and I have dealt with these in the preceding section.

Life-size garden statues used in dissimilar ways. The female figure in an opening in a dense hedge is dramatic against the light on the landscape behind her. The male figure is in a romantic, wild setting.

A fine cast iron statuette flanked by a bower of roses at Sutton Park.

This statue at Belvoir Castle is one of six fine figures by Caius Cibber, sculptor to Charles II.

Left and far left. Fine 18th century animal groups flank the private parterre at Chatsworth.

Far left. Plaster copy of the cast iron dogs at St. George's, Hanover Square, labradors originally cast in 1840.

Left. An Italian Renaissance model, cast in Coadestone in the early 19th century, now at Swyncombe House.

Pan surveys a pool at Rousham, Oxfordshire.

Statue on pedestal at Buscot.

Elegant stone feature at Easton Grey, Malmesbury.

A fine late 18th century urn and pedestal in front of a manicured yew hedge at Hidcote.

Massive pot at Noordhoek, the Cape, South Africa.

Overflowing container at Knightshayes Court.

In their all-green garden, Mr. and Mrs. Feilding allowed colour only in pairs of pots by doorways and openings in hedges.

Left. This old kitchen sink makes a delightful container for miniature plants, and forms with the other flower pots the sort of pleasing arrangement which anybody can achieve.

Far left. Alistair McAlpine commissioned Quinlan Terry to design this column for the end of an avenue at West Green House. Built in stone, it must be the finest garden ornament of our age.

Above. Pair of terracotta pots at Stellenberg, South Africa.

Right. Round terracotta pot on pedestal at Cliveden.

Below left. A watchful heron at The Manor House, Bledlow.

Below right. This engaging piece is a particular favourite of mine.

THE DEMISE OF DAVID HICKS

My father had almost completed this book when he died on Sunday, 29 March 1998. It was only four days since the whole family had taken him out for what he told us was 'the best birthday ever', a dinner at 7p.m. sharp at L'Incontro, consisting only of oysters. He had been in amazing form, springing up to greet old friends with a shout, giving no one a clue that he was dying.

The night before he died he was faxing instructions to Dana for the last remaining photographs, planning and organising to the last. The next morning he was too weak to get up. His dear old friend the Dowager Lady Hesketh arrived for lunch with a posy of wild flowers from her garden, and I read him some pages from the memoirs of Princess Alice, Duchess of Gloucester. He smiled at the description of how the gravel outside the Buccleuch house was raked by the four outside men every day, whether it was driven on or not.

He died in his bed, looking out of the window at his beloved garden, which was just beginning to bloom with the first warmth of spring, his eyes going from his lines of stilt trees, now so splendidly mature, to the clouds scudding across the blue sky.

After he was gone, we found his little white book, 'The Demise of David Hicks', written out by hand some ten years before, and constantly updated, detailing every moment of his funeral and memorial service. There was a great rush to get his flag made, and the trailer built and 'strewn with ivy' as instructed, and the coffin made, in the grey-stained sycamore that he had specified, absolutely plain except for his H-logo in pewter ('handles are so common') and lined with his own fabric.

He lay until the funeral in the bottom room of the Pavilion, designed for that purpose. On the Saturday he was carried out, across the little drawbridge, through the garden, out of the gate, where we placed him on the ivy-strewn trailer behind his own Range Rover, its painted steel flag up for the last journey.

Liking the interior of Ewelme church but the graveyard at Brightwell Baldwin, and having always enjoyed a good procession, he had elected to have the service in one church and the burial at the other, so that a seemingly unending line of cars stretched behind him, filling the back and front drives of The Grove, winding slowly past his beloved garden in a final tour led by the Master.

On the first day of July 1998, in the little Grosvenor Chapel behind which he had lived as a young art student in London, we had his Memorial Service. With Richard Barratt's help we constructed two towering, slender pyramids covered in oak leaves stripped from the many trees he had planted, interwoven with his favourite roses from The Grove. They filled the chapel with such a scent that it was like walking into his Secret Garden with him still there, showing off like mad, loving every minute of it.

Ashley Hicks, April 1999

The view from David Hicks' bed at The Grove. He moved the bed some months before he died so as to be closer to the window and have a better view of the clipped hornbeams he loved so much. The washbasin is set extremely low, so as not to obstruct the view.

INDEX